RUTH, ESTHER
ECCLESIASTES
SONG OF SONGS
— *and* —
LAMENTATIONS

Text copyright © Robert Fyall 2005

The author asserts the moral right to be
identified as the author of this work

Published by
The Bible Reading Fellowship
First Floor, Elsfield Hall
15–17 Elsfield Way, Oxford OX2 8FG
ISBN 1 84101 242 4

First published 2005
10 9 8 7 6 5 4 3 2 1 0

Acknowledgments
Unless otherwise stated, scripture quotations are taken from
the Holy Bible, New International Version, copyright © 1973, 1978, 1984 by
International Bible society. Used by permission of Hodder & Stoughton Ltd.
All rights reserved. 'NIV' is a registered trademark of International Bible
Society. UK trademark number 1448790.

Scripture quotations from The Revised Standard Version of the Bible, copyright
© 1946, 1952, 1971 by the Division of Christian Education of the National
Council of the Churches of Christ in the United States of America, are used by
permission. All rights reserved.

A catalogue record for this book is
available from the British Library

Printed and bound in Great Britain
by Bookmarque, Croydon

RUTH, ESTHER ECCLESIASTES SONG OF SONGS *and* LAMENTATIONS

THE PEOPLE'S BIBLE COMMENTARY

ROBERT FYALL

A BIBLE COMMENTARY FOR EVERY DAY

Acknowledgments

Grateful thanks to Naomi Starkey, Commissioning Editor of BRF for inviting me to write this book and bearing patiently with the many delays as successive deadlines passed. As always my family have provided the context of love and support in which the work was done, so thanks to my now grown-up children; Carmen and Drummond, and above all to my wife, Thelma. Many thanks as well to Carol Fry, formerly Senior Church Worker at Claypath Church, Durham and to Andrew Kelman on the staff of Rutherford House, Edinburgh for transferring my script to disc.

Introducing the
People's Bible Commentary
series

Congratulations! You are embarking on a voyage of discovery—or rediscovery. You may feel you know the Bible very well; you may never have turned its pages before. You may be looking for a fresh way of approaching daily Bible study; you may be searching for useful insights to share in a study group or from a pulpit.

The People's Bible Commentary (PBC) series is designed for all those who want to study the scriptures in a way that will warm the heart as well as instructing the mind. To help you, the series distils the best of scholarly insights into the straightforward language and devotional emphasis of Bible reading notes. Explanation of background material, and discussion of the original Greek and Hebrew, will always aim to be brief.

- If you have never really studied the Bible before, the series offers a serious yet accessible way in.

- If you help to lead a church study group, or are otherwise involved in regular preaching and teaching, you can find invaluable 'snapshots' of a Bible passage through the PBC approach.

- If you are a church worker or minister, burned out on the Bible, this series could help you recover the wonder of scripture.

Using a People's Bible Commentary

The series is designed for use alongside any version of the Bible. You may have your own favourite translation, but you might like to consider trying a different one in order to gain fresh perspectives on familiar passages.

Many Bible translations come in a range of editions, including study and reference editions that have concordances, various kinds of special index, maps and marginal notes. These can all prove helpful in studying the relevant passage. The Notes section at the back of each PBC volume provides space for you to write personal reflections, points to follow up, questions and comments.

Each People's Bible Commentary can be used on a daily basis, instead of Bible reading notes. Alternatively, it can be read straight through, or used as a resource book for insight into particular verses of the biblical book.

If you have enjoyed using this commentary and would like to progress further in Bible study, you will find details of other volumes in the series listed at the back, together with information about a special offer from BRF.

While it is important to deepen understanding of a given passage, this series always aims to engage both heart and mind in the study of the Bible. The scriptures point to our Lord himself and our task is to use them to build our relationship with him. When we read, let us do so prayerfully, slowly, reverently, expecting him to speak to our hearts.

CONTENTS

PBC RUTH, ESTHER, ECCLESIASTES, SONG OF SONGS & LAMENTATIONS: INTRODUCTION

Five little books are the subject of this commentary and all of them contain interest and difficulty disproportionate to their size. Two of them are stories set in the wider framework of biblical history (Ruth and Esther); one is a puzzling Wisdom book (Ecclesiastes); one is a national lament (Lamentations) and one is a love poem (Song of Songs). Some of them were the subject of fierce debate over whether they should be in the canon of scripture or not. To help us to get our bearings, we shall ask some basic questions.

Where?

Where are they in the Bible? In our English Bibles they are placed either in the historical period to which they refer or with the type of literature with which they are most naturally associated. Thus Ruth, set in the days of the Judges and pointing towards David, comes between Judges and Samuel. Esther, a story set in Persia and dealing with the exiles who remained there, comes after Ezra and Nehemiah. Lamentations, traditionally ascribed to Jeremiah, follows that prophet's book. Ecclesiastes and the Song of Songs stand next to the other Wisdom books of Job and Proverbs.

In the Hebrew Bible, however, the five books stand together in the third section, known as the Writings (the first two sections being the Law and the Prophets—all three together form the Old Testament). They were adopted as lectionary readings for major festivals and came collectively to be known as the Five Scrolls. These festivals are Passover (springtime: Song of Songs); Feast of Weeks or Pentecost (50 days later—associated with the wheat harvest: Ruth); Ninth of Ab (late summer—anniversary of the fall of Jerusalem: Lamentations); Feast of Booths or Tabernacles (late September: Ecclesiastes); Feast of Purim (end of year: Esther). Four of these are festivals of rejoicing at God's goodness in creation and history, and one (Ninth of Ab) is a lament for the great national disaster of the exile.

What?

These books are all difficult and many of them seem to sit uneasily with the rest of the Bible. Many of the issues are dealt with as they arise in the following pages of this commentary, but a few words would be useful here. Song of Songs appears to be a completely sensual love poem and this has led many over the centuries to find allegorical meanings. Ruth appears to be a straightforward story, but, as we shall see, it is a subtle book with many ambiguities. Lamentations is hard and painful as it wrestles with the greatest catastrophe in Israel's biblical history. Esther does not mention God and seems an unedifying story. Ecclesiastes is relentless in its exposure of sham and unreality.

Yet these books have not been edited out of the canon; they each have something distinctive that we need to hear. They all grapple with big issues and must be seen in the context of the Bible as a whole. Other matters of background and origin will be dealt with as appropriate in the individual commentaries.

Why?

What is the distinctive value and contribution of these books? Five points can be made.

First, these books come to us from the fringes of the biblical canon and, as such, explore the relationship between the edges and the centre of biblical theology. There is history, but it is rather far away from the mainstream. In one sense the story of Esther is central, dealing with the near destruction of the Jewish race, but the lack of reference to Israel's earlier history and institutions gives it a rather odd feel. The whole sacrificial and ritual life of ancient Israel is barely mentioned there. Ecclesiastes, in particular, says things that seem to deviate from mainstream orthodoxy. Closer reading in the light of the rest of scripture shows that there is a two-way process at work, and reveals much we would otherwise have missed—for example, the echoes of Exodus in Esther and the Psalter in Lamentations. On the other hand, in Ruth and (in a different way) in the Song of Songs we find a more personal look at the great story which is the Bible's plot-line.

Second, their setting in the context of community worship (the five major festivals) reminds us that scripture shapes worship and must be heard in the context of praise, thanksgiving and confession. Scripture prevents worship from being simply our private ideas about

God. Those ancient festivals are important reminders of God's mighty acts in time and space, and the Five Scrolls powerfully bring out the essence of these celebrations.

Third, these books have profound pastoral implications. They take us into a world of intense joy and massive grief. They use genres such as story, poetry, proverb and lament, which run the whole gamut of human emotions. They do not have the grandeur of the great prophets, the narrative excitement of the David story or the profundities of the Psalms, but they throw light into unexpected corners and sound notes hardly heard elsewhere. Read carefully, for example, chapters 2 and 3 of Ruth and see how a love story in a provincial town perfectly illustrates the tension between divine providence and human responsibility. Wrestle with Lamentations' anatomy of grieving, and question the anomalies of life with Ecclesiastes.

Fourth, while commenting on the Five Scrolls together, we need to remember that each has its own distinctive style, emphasis and contribution. The atmosphere of each is different: the springtime of love in the Song of Songs, the pastoral maturity of Ruth, the bitter communal grief of Lamentations, the autumnal chill of Ecclesiastes and the exotic splendour of Esther. The theological emphases are varied as well, from Ruth's easy fit into the mainstream of Davidic history to the Song of Songs' echoes of Genesis 1 and 2 and Ecclesiastes' ambiguous relationship with Proverbs.

Fifth, these books need to be seen in the context of the whole Bible and not simply Old Testament theology. They are part of the written word that points to the living Word, Jesus Christ himself. So this commentary will be careful to point out how, sometimes very indirectly, these books bear witness to the gospel.

I pray that this commentary will be of help to all who read it, in helping them to understand these neglected parts of the Bible. I also hope it will be of use to those who teach and preach. I have preached through each of these books, some more than once, and, while this is a commentary and not a series of sermons, it has sprung from engaging with the problems and possibilities of expounding the text to others.

Further reading

There are many commentaries on these books and I have included only a brief selection from those I found especially helpful in my own study.

The Five Scrolls

Eugene H. Peterson, *Five Smooth Stones for Pastoral Work* (Eerdmans/Gracewing, 1980)

Barry G. Webb, *Five Festal Garments* (Apollos, IVP, 2000)

Song of Songs

T. Gledhill, *The Message of the Song of Songs* (BST, IVP, 1994).

Tremper Longman III, *Song of Songs* (New International Commentary on the Old Testament, 2001).

Roland Murphy, *The Song of Songs* (Hermeneia, 1990).

Ruth

Fredric Bush, *Ruth/Esther* (Word Biblical Commentary, 1996).

Tod Linafelte, *Ruth, Esther* (Timothy K. Beal, Berit Olam, 1999)

R.L. Hubbard, *The Book of Ruth* (New International Commentary on the Old Testament, 1988).

Lamentations

J. Andrew Dearman, *Jeremiah/Lamentations* (NIV Application Commentary, 2002)

Robert Gordis, *The Song of Songs and Lamentations* (Ktav, 3rd Edn., 1994)

Ecclesiastes

Michael A. Eaton, *Ecclesiastes* (Tyndale Commentaries, IVP, 1983)

Iain Provan, *Ecclesiastes/Song of Songs* (NIV Application Commentary. 2001)

Esther

Joyce G. Baldwin, *Esther* (Tyndale Commentaries, IVP, 1984)

Karen H. Jobes, *Esther* (NIV Application Commentary, 1999)

Dianne Tidball, *Esther: A True First Lady* (Christian Focus, 2001)

TWO FUNERALS & *a* FAMINE

Here we begin one of the Bible's most beautiful and sensitive stories and we must first pause to get our bearings and ask what kind of story it is. We have two clues—firstly that it is one of the Five Scrolls sung at the great festivals of Israel. It was assigned to be read at Pentecost along with the story of the giving of the Law at Sinai, and thus this little tale becomes part of the great story of God's salvation of his people. It is about how God relates to his people and how they relate to him.

The second clue is that it happened 'when the judges ruled' (v. 1). In our English Bible it follows the chaotic and bloodthirsty story of Judges 19—21 and is a vivid contrast to it. The setting of the book in the period of the Judges tells us nothing of where or by whom it was written. Some have argued for a post-exilic date and seen parallels with the stringent marriage policies of Ezra and Nehemiah (Ezra 10; Nehemiah 13). The book notably lacks a polemical tone, however, and there are no obvious allusions to the post-exilic period. A more likely time is the reign of David or perhaps Solomon, when foreigners were a large part of the power base; as Ruth is a fine example of a foreigner who commits herself to Israel and to Yahweh.

The story

Ruth is a gentle book and the world of Judges 19—21 could hardly be more different. Bethlehem, where the story begins, is the place in Judges 19 where a girl is snatched, gang-raped and dumped at the door of her pimp, who then cuts up her body and sends the parts round Israel. Violence is compounded by famine, and a situation arises like those occurring in recent years in the Horn of Africa, if not exactly caused, then exacerbated by the activities of local warlords. Ironically, Bethlehem means 'house of bread'.

All the ingredients are here for another story of violence and death. Indeed, the first few verses appear to bear out this expectation. Naomi, on whom these verses centre, loses her husband and her two sons in an almost Job-like experience. Apart from the appalling personal loss and grief, her economic support has gone and she is an alien in a land to which she had gone a decade before with such high hopes.

The characters

Names were given to children in Old Testament times in order to express a hope and prayer that the child would live up to its name. Elimelech means 'My God is King', and it is difficult to argue that he had lived up to his parents' expectations. Also, where would Marlon and Kilion find Jewish girls to marry in Moab?

These three hapless men appear in the narrative only to marry and die. Far more energy and spiritual insight is to be shown by the women in the story. In verses 6–7, all the verbs are singular: the return to Judah is Naomi's initiative. She is the moving spirit; she decides to go back to her spiritual roots and to connect her story with God's story.

The outcome

Verse 6 includes a ringing challenge to cynicism and despair: the Lord had 'visited' his people (RSV). 'Visited' is one of the great biblical words of God's intervention; it is not simply that he happened to be passing, rather that he has come with a purpose. Here, that purpose is blessing: Bethlehem is once again to live up to its name and be a 'house of bread'. For Elimelech and his sons, the journey to Moab was to death and oblivion. For Naomi and her daughters-in-law, the road runs not only back to Judah but into the future. How bright and glorious that future would turn out to be could hardly have been guessed. Indeed it was not to be truly fulfilled until, at another time of darkness, Zechariah exclaimed in awe and wonder that the Lord had come and visited his people (Luke 1:68).

In a few swift strokes, our author has set the scene, introduced characters and created a sense of expectancy. The story appears to have a kind of artless simplicity but, as we shall see, this hides a very subtle plot and shrewd characterization. This storyteller misses nothing. Even characters who appear only to disappear are named. This anchors the story in reality. It is not about 'a certain man' and 'a certain woman'. It both begins and ends with a cluster of names that frame the narrative. In this book God is going to address each of us by name; it is going to be both exhilarating and terrifying.

PRAYER
Lord, you know each of us by name and are with us throughout good and bad days. May our stories be part of the great story and our lives be fruitful for you.

PAINFUL CONVERSATIONS

So far, no one has spoken a word; the style has been terse and the emotion generated by the starkness of the events themselves. Now our author not only pushes the story forward but also draws us into the inner lives of Naomi and Ruth by means of three moving and poignant conversations. We begin with Naomi breaking the long silence.

Where is home?

First, Naomi tries formally to release her daughters-in-law from any obligations they may feel towards her. There is urgency in her voice as she tries to persuade them. The phrase 'mother's home' (v. 8) in place of the more normal 'father's home' may underline the helplessness of the women without male protection or a recognizable role in society.

Most striking in this first conversation, however, is the introduction of themes that are important for the book and for the Old Testament as a whole. We find the great Hebrew word *hesed*, translated as 'kindness' (v. 8). This is the word particularly used of God's love to his people with whom he is in covenant relationship. Thus in Exodus 20:6 God is the one who shows such love from generation to generation. It is startling evidence that God's grace has already been at work in a story so far marked by death and tragedy.

Moreover, by committing Ruth and Orpah to the blessing of Yahweh, Naomi is stating her belief that Yahweh has authority outside Israel. His blessing and his guidance know no national boundaries.

All this hitherto suppressed emotion expresses itself in weeping (v. 9) and the three women are joined in a circle of shared memories as they face an uncertain future. Where is to be home for these three?

An impossible scenario

Once again Naomi speaks (v. 11), setting up an impossible scenario. Even if she were to produce more sons, there would be no possibility of Ruth and Orpah waiting to marry them. This means that only Yahweh can do anything, but just what that might be is beyond Naomi's grieving imagination. In verse 13 she blames God directly for the misfortunes that she has endured. This is important because she is realizing that God alone rules in the universe but, like Job, she fears that he has become hostile and wishes her ill. This will call for further comment when we come to 1:21.

A second outburst of weeping closes this conversation and leads to two decisive actions: Orpah leaves, but Ruth is determined to stay with Naomi (v. 14). The narrator makes no judgment on Orpah but she passes from the story without a word and we hear no more of her.

A lifelong commitment

While Naomi begins a third conversation (v. 15), it is Ruth who dominates it. Naomi begins with a reminder that Ruth's and Orpah's identity and heartland ('her people and her gods') have been bound up with Moab and thus she urges Ruth to return there.

Ruth's reply (vv. 16–17) is lyrical and passionate and represents an astonishing leap of faith and depth of commitment. Like Abraham, she is going to leave all the familiar certainties and launch into the unknown. Her commitment is first to Naomi but it will go far beyond that. The commitment is permanent: not only will she go with Naomi but 'where you stay I will stay'. She will renounce her roots and her former people: 'your people will be my people'. More striking still, in spite of Naomi's bitter complaint against Yahweh (v. 13), she will build her hopes on that same God. This commitment will be sealed by her being placed to rest among her new people when her death comes. Ruth underlines the total seriousness of her intentions by making an oath in Yahweh's name (v. 17).

It is difficult for us, in a highly mobile society with few allegiances and frequent house moves, to appreciate the radical nature of what Ruth promises and carries out. Yet this is nothing more or less than the radical obedience Christ expects from his followers in every age. More than that, the similarity already noted with Abraham's story gives Ruth's story a sense of destiny. Who knows what will happen when we start out on the great pilgrimage of faith?

Verse 18 brings the dialogue to a close and introduces the next stage of the story. Ruth's determination is, in human terms, to be the driving force in the succeeding episode.

REFLECTION

Apparently simple choices may lead to momentous consequences.
The life of faith calls us to make definite choices and open-ended
commitments. We never know exactly what God has in store for us.

An UNHAPPY ARRIVAL

This passage is brief but of great importance. The journey to Bethlehem is completed for both women. For Naomi it is the return to a place once familiar and now very different. For Ruth it is the beginning of a severe test of faith. Naomi, far from welcoming and introducing Ruth to her new home, sidelines her, behaving and talking as if she were not there (vv. 20–21).

Being honest about God

Once again, powerful emotions well up. The narrator does not make clear exactly what stirred the townspeople so deeply, but their emphasis on her name causes Naomi to burst out in passionate lament. She repudiates that name which means 'pleasant' or 'lovely', and suggests Mara ('bitterness') as far more appropriate for her situation. Yahweh is supposed to be especially the protector of widows (see Exodus 22:22–24), but her bitterness is particularly related to her unhappiness in losing husband and sons. 'Empty' is emphatic: 'it was empty that Yahweh brought me back'. The gift of Ruth's loyalty is forgotten in this moment of despair.

Once again, as in verse 13 but with greater emphasis, Naomi traces all the disasters directly to the action of God. The name 'Almighty' is often associated with God as cosmic overlord and ruler of destinies (see Numbers 24:4; Psalm 68:14; Job 11:7; 27:13; 31:2). Like Job, Naomi is in no doubt as to where the responsibility lies for all that happens. (This will also mean that, when God restores her fortunes, he alone will deserve the praise.)

Naomi's lament implies an honesty and lack of pretence on her part: she stands before God and wants to know the answer. Moreover, the juxtaposition of the name Yahweh and the title 'Almighty' in verses 20–21 is a key to understanding something of what is happening. 'Almighty' used on its own could easily suggest a remote and un-concerned God, living light years away and unaffected by the experi-ences of village life. 'Yahweh' is the Lord of the covenant, however, committed to his people by promises that he will not and cannot break. His promises often are mysterious and his ways perplexing, yet we know that ultimately he will work everything together for good.

Getting our bearings

Before we find out how the story is going to develop, the narrator gives us a very carefully crafted summary of where we are, as well as hints of where we are going (v. 22).

Strictly speaking, it is only Naomi who has 'returned', since Ruth has never been to Bethlehem before. The strong suggestion, however, is that Ruth 'the Moabitess' has now found her true home. Some commentators have found this puzzling and inconsistent because it appears to breach the statutes of Deuteronomy 23:3–6, which prohibit Moabites from entering the assembly of Yahweh, but this is to take too narrow a view. Yahweh, the protector of widows, has called Ruth to be part of his own people, and she has responded positively. In the genealogy of Jesus in Matthew 1, Ruth is linked with that other outsider, Rahab, who, as a Canaanite, should also have been excluded from Israel. So here we have a wonderful example of the grace of God. We have already noted the similarity of Ruth's commitment to that of Abraham, and we remember that he was called so that all nations on earth would be blessed (Genesis 12:3). We also remember that love is the fulfilment of the Law (Romans 13:10).

The narrator is concerned to tell us the precise time that the two women arrived in Bethlehem. The chapter began with a famine but ends at the beginning of the barley harvest, which was late April/early May. Food is going to be plentiful and the Lord of the harvest is not going to abandon the two widows. The famine at the beginning was accompanied by death; perhaps this harvest is the forerunner of new life. We end chapter 1 on a more hopeful note than we began it, and we anticipate God doing something new and surprising.

PRAYER

Lord God, your ways are mysterious and your purposes beyond our understanding. Yet we know that you love us and that in your good time you bring a harvest. Help us to trust you through the dark moments and wait in hope and faith for the dawn. Amen.

ENTER BOAZ

By now we have become familiar with the flow of the book: swift, clear narrative sketches and dialogues which reveal character as well as carrying on the story. This pattern continues in chapter 2, yet there is a significant difference. Chapter 1 hurries over circumstances that took a decade to unfold; chapter 2 lingers lovingly over the events of one sunny day. That in itself is significant in the developing theology of Ruth. Length of time is no indication of importance. While all time belongs to God and is significant, a short and decisive episode can accomplish what years failed to do. Such an episode is our concern in this chapter.

First moves

The chapter opens with a hint that Naomi's emptiness might not be as total as it appears to be. Here again our author shows great skill. Boaz' name is introduced at the very end of the sentence, thus building suspense. We are given a glimpse here of the social structure of the old Israel. The 'clan' was a unit between the family and the larger tribe, consisting of families descended from a common ancestor. Joshua 13—19 outlines how lands were divided out among various clans. Thus Boaz' 'fullness' (in the sense of his wealth and standing, is a contrast to Naomi's 'emptiness'. The description 'man of standing' (v. 1) most often denotes a warrior, but that nuance is absent here—except, probably, that this is a man under whose protection the weak would be safe. None of this, however, is known to Ruth at this point.

Ruth again makes a decisive move—and a wise one, because the harvest might only last a matter of days. The right to glean was guaranteed by the law (Leviticus 19:9–10; 23:22; Deuteronomy 24:19–24), because Yahweh himself is the owner of the land. Once again Ruth is called 'the Moabitess' (v. 2), reminding us of her double vulnerability as a widow and a foreigner and thus her need of protection. Her words show a fine blend of courage and humility and illustrate the great significance of human character and choices. We are about to see the interplay of this with divine providence.

God behind the scenes

Verse 3 encapsulates that providence neatly. Ruth goes into the fields and begins to work; we could be reading a simple story of village life. Then, 'as it turned out', she finds herself in a field belonging to none other than Boaz. The phrase translated 'as it turned out' is a hint that Yahweh is at work behind the scenes. It occurs in contexts where events happen without human contrivance or intention. The Lord of the harvest is at work here.

God's resourcefulness

These three verses are of great importance in the book, and there are a number of ways in which they can speak into our situation. First, we are reminded of God's continual resourcefulness. Presumably, in her grief and bitterness, Naomi had forgotten about Boaz or, if she remembered him, felt that he could or would do nothing to help. God is not limited by our lack of resources; nor is he ever without solutions, whether we can see them or not.

Second, there is an important part to be played by human resourcefulness. Ruth's initiative and enterprise are key factors, which put her in the right place to take advantage of Yahweh's provision. Boaz was there but Ruth needed to go to the field and do the work in order to meet him.

Third, God's provision and our human response to it belong together. We have neither a rigid determinism, which reduces humans to puppets, nor a human-centred universe where God is little more than an emergency helpline. Rather, God works in and through our universe and interacts with rational beings made in his image.

None of this means that life will be straightforward: we have reached this point in the story after death, exile, sorrow and bitterness. Rather, it means that what we call 'coincidence' is in fact a particular example of God's providence working in ways plain to him but not to us. It would help our walk with God considerably if we were to look at apparently trivial happenings in this way.

PRAYER

Lord, so often we find life perplexing and confusing. There seems little pattern or meaning in events as they happen. Help us to trust you when we cannot see, and to believe that you are working for our good and our blessing. Amen.

FINDING FAVOUR

Having successfully caught our interest, the author now brings Boaz himself on to the scene and there follows the first meeting and conversation between him and Ruth. Ruth, it appears, has come not only to the right field but also at the right time.

Getting to know one another

Two things emerge from Boaz' first words. First, we notice his courtesy to the reapers (v. 4). Some men in his position would have loftily ignored them. Instead, not only does Boaz greet them but he wishes them the presence of Yahweh. This is no mere conventional greeting but an underlining of God's involvement in all aspects of life and work. Thus the underlying thread of the story is made explicit. The sense of God's involvement in the most ordinary of circumstances is an important feature of the theology of the book.

Second, Boaz inquires about Ruth (v. 5) and receives a lengthy reply, which succinctly reminds us of the issues of chapter 1. Her foreign status, her care for Naomi, her courtesy and her diligence are all crisply outlined in verse 6. Moreover, the foreman is briefly glimpsed as a generous individual, giving Ruth the credit and speaking well of her. In the vicinity of Boaz there is an atmosphere of generosity.

This becomes explicit in the conversation between Boaz and Ruth. 'My daughter' (v. 8) suggests that Boaz is rather older than Ruth; probably he is a contemporary of Naomi. He is anxious that she stay; this is shown by the repetition: 'Don't go and glean in another field and don't go away from here.' He effectively takes Ruth under his protection by guaranteeing her work, preventing amorous males from touching her, and looking after her physical needs by giving her water (v. 9).

What is he up to?

Boaz' motives are not made clear, and some commentators have seen him as a rich, predatory older man taking advantage of a young and helpless girl. This view cannot be supported from the text. Far from taking advantage of her, he provides protection, and he does not make a pass at her. We need not deny, however, that he is probably attracted to her and thus anxious to get to know her better.

More significant is the generosity of Boaz. The law forbids ill-treatment of strangers (Exodus 22:21), but Boaz goes far beyond the letter of the law and shows positive kindness, as God himself does (see 1:8). There is a richness and abundance in Boaz' generosity that corresponds to the physical abundance of the harvest.

Ruth, for her part, responds to this generosity with humility and gratitude (v. 10). Her modesty and deference are a fitting counterpart to such sudden and unexpected blessings.

God's kindness

In verse 11 we have a little more of the background filled in. Boaz is effectively treating Ruth as she has treated Naomi. Once again his words are more than conventional pleasantries. Ruth's leaving of parents and homeland echoes similar phrases used of Abraham (Genesis 12:1; 24:7) and of Jacob (Genesis 31:13). Ruth's story is again being linked with that of Israel's ancestors. Like them, she is to be protected by Yahweh, the Lord of the covenant. 'Wings' (v. 12) suggests tenderness as well as protection. Moreover, Boaz is careful to underline the source of the generosity: 'May the Lord repay you.' This is no mere tale of rustic life; it is part of the great epic of the Lord's generosity to Israel, which is to be the channel for his blessing to the whole world.

In Ruth's reply in verse 13 she designates herself as a servant and yet shows a mature judgment of the situation and points forward to a developing relationship. Boaz' generosity has evoked a fitting response which is neither servile nor indifferent.

It is worth reflecting on how this episode has advanced the story. Boaz is seen to be fully deserving of his reputation and Ruth continues to make the favourable impression already seen in chapter 1, yet we do not feel that we are encountering impossibly good individuals. Rather, both are marked by shrewdness and initiative. Both clearly wish their association to continue and suspense is built up as we await the next development.

PRAYER

Lord God, you know us better than we know ourselves; our lives are in your hand and you are committed to us by promises that you cannot and will not break. Give us faith to trust you in the everyday circumstances of our lives and to believe that you are working everything for good. Amen.

A MEAL & ITS AFTERMATH

Ruth's acceptance into the community continues with a shared meal. This meal, like all else, is no meagre rations; abundant and generous provision is lavished on Ruth (v. 14). Here we have a complete reversal of the famine of the first chapter, which set the whole sad story in motion. In individual lives the reality of 1:6 is illustrated: 'The Lord had come to the aid of his people by providing food for them.' Here at work is the Lord of the harvest, the extravagantly generous giver who does not simply meet the need but gives much more. Here is the Lord in whose hands a few loaves became an overwhelming harvest with loaves left over (Luke 9:12–17). Here is grace which, where sin increases, increases much more (Romans 5:10).

Abundant generosity

The generosity characteristic of the meal continues into the subsequent work. Boaz allows Ruth access to the area between the sheaves (vv. 15–16). Gleaners would not normally have had such access because owners would wish to keep any grain dropped for themselves. Once again, this goes well beyond the letter of the law. Deuteronomy 24:19 tells reapers not to return for dropped grain, but Boaz is positively encouraging the widow to collect such grain rather than simply leaving it for her. But even yet he is not finished. In verse 16 he instructs his workers deliberately to pull out grain and leave it for Ruth to pick up.

This story is a real one about real people, not an allegory with concealed spiritual lessons, yet it is a window into something bigger and greater. This tale of two widows and a generous man is an acted parable of the great story of God's love and generosity, which comes to us in our alienation and vulnerability and welcomes us into his house and family.

Ruth takes initiatives, behaves with modesty and earns the admiration of the reader as well as that of Boaz. Indeed, Ruth's industry corresponds to Boaz' generosity. The amount she collected is described as an 'ephah' (v. 17): about 22 litres. Some have argued that this means Ruth collected the equivalent of at least two weeks' wages in one day. She and Naomi would have no fear now about food. Boaz' wish in 2:12 that the Lord would repay Ruth has been spectacularly fulfilled.

Beyond the harvest

The scene now shifts back to Naomi's home (v. 19), resuming the conversation of 2:2. Naomi is plainly astonished by the provision Ruth has brought. Again, the great covenant word *hesed* is used and applied to Boaz (v. 20). This is another indication that behind this generosity is that of the Lord himself.

Also, Boaz is described as a 'kinsman-redeemer', an important term for the rest of the book. The term *go'el* comes from the family laws of old Israel. The *go'el* was responsible for repurchasing property once owned by clan members but lost through economic difficulties (Leviticus 25:25–30). If relatives were enslaved by poverty, he would try to buy them back (Leviticus 25:47–55). Thus Boaz has duties towards Naomi and Ruth. His conduct has already shown that not only will he fulfil these obligations but he will go well beyond them.

Verse 21 again refers to Ruth as 'the Moabitess', thus underlining the broadmindedness of Boaz. The verse also brings further suspense as a temporal note is introduced: 'until they finish harvesting'. This reminds us of the continual need for reliance on the Lord of the harvest rather than on the harvest itself. This is reinforced by Naomi's words in verse 22, which end with a warning to look out for possible harm.

This delightful chapter closes with a summary note by the narrator; in verse 23 the warning note already mentioned occurs again. This is the end of the harvest and who knows what lies beyond it? The barley and wheat harvests make up the entire harvest period, the seven or so weeks from late April to early June. The words 'she lived with her mother-in-law' suggest a passing of time and uneventfulness after a crowded and memorable day. The abiding impression in this chapter is of the bountiful generosity of Yahweh mediated through Boaz, yet Ruth still has no home of her own and there is a need for faith and probably further risk-taking.

MEDITATION

You care for the land and water it; you enrich it abundantly. The streams of God are filled with water to provide the people with corn... You crown the year with your bounty, and your carts overflow with abundance.

Psalm 65:9–11

A DARING PLAN

With chapter 3 we reach the turning point of the book, which takes place over a single night. Once again the story is carried forward by both dialogue and action. There are many ambiguities and cross-currents here and we shall have to listen carefully to the text.

Naomi's initiative

It is Naomi who takes the initiative, and her emphasis is very clearly on marriage and the security that it will bring. Back in chapter 1, her 'emptiness' consisted of both the loss of her husband and the effects of the famine. Famine had been replaced by plenty in chapter 2 but still the security of marriage and descendants (longed for in 1:8-9) remains elusive. Now Naomi is going to seize the opportunity of the emergence of Boaz on to the scene.

Winnowing was the climax of the harvest, and it was a festive occasion. Threshing floors became linked in the popular mind with licentiousness (hence the reference in Hosea 9:1). Commentators who make much of this are probably reading too much into the text, however. The fact that many who attended these end-of-harvest parties behaved in a drunken and sexually provocative manner does not mean that everyone behaved in that way. We have to ask—as we do throughout this chapter—whether such behaviour is implied here, given the characters of Ruth and Boaz as they have emerged.

Ruth is not simply to rush into an encounter with Boaz but rather to wait until he has finished eating. Then she is to 'uncover his feet' (v. 4). Once again the phrase has sexual overtones in some contexts, and the word 'feet' can be used to refer to the sexual organs (see, for example, Exodus 4:25). That does not mean that such a nuance is present here. Nevertheless the whole procedure is risky and fraught with all kinds of possibilities for disaster.

A brief summary verse (v. 6) provides a rapid transition to the crucial scene, simultaneously underlining Ruth's obedience and heightening suspense. The story unfolds in swift, telling and memorable phrases with an ambivalence that we have already noted. Thus, 'when Boaz had finished eating and drinking and was in good spirits'

(v. 7) need not mean that he was drunk but rather that he was mellow and relaxed—a good time to approach him.

We can only imagine Ruth's nervousness; we almost hear her breathing and the beat of her heart. The wording of verse 7 follows exactly that of verse 4, which both further emphasizes Ruth's obedience and raises the tension: it does sound a very odd plan.

God at work

The story so far is fascinating, but what are we to make of it, theologically and practically? One important factor is the difference between these verses and the previous chapter. In chapter 2 the initiative was God's, and we discussed the significant phrase 'as it turned out' (2:3). Here God is very much in the background and the initiative is in the hands of the main human characters. It is only by reading these chapters in tandem that we will discern the sophistication and depth of the narrative. Chapter 2, taken on its own, could suggest that human actions and attitudes are relatively insignificant and that we are simply pawns in a cosmic game. Chapter 3, taken alone, could suggest that humans have total control over what happens. By placing them together, however, our author shows the sovereignty of God interacting with the responsibility of humans to grasp opportunities and take initiatives. Nowhere is this put more starkly than in Philippians 2:12–13: 'Continue to work out your salvation with fear and trembling, for it is God who works in you to will and to act according to his good purpose.'

Sometimes God will guide in a very direct, even spectacular way. For most of our lives, just as for the characters of this book, guidance is more evident when we look back. Here it is related especially to grasping opportunities, taking risks and making plans which may or may not work out. Certainty is not possible, and openness to God and his prompting is necessary.

PRAYER

Lord, make us so sensitive to your guidance that when we act
it will be you acting in and through us. Amen.

A NIGHT-TIME ENCOUNTER

At midnight the critical moment approaches. This time is often significant in scripture: it is the moment of the Israelites leaving Egypt in Exodus 12 and the return of the Bridegroom in Matthew 25. Here Boaz, an upright and highly respected pillar of the community, finds himself alone in the small hours with an attractive and—as he thinks—unknown young woman. Again, an atmosphere of tension is built up. 'The man' and 'a woman' (v. 8) give a sense of mystery and the scene takes place in darkness. The total lack of our knowledge of the actual emotions of the main characters further adds to the depth of the scene. The background is in shadow; no crowds of reapers or villagers stroll past as the spotlight plays on the two main characters.

What follows in verse 9 departs from the script. Naomi had said that Boaz would tell Ruth what to do (3:4), but here Ruth takes the initiative and, in effect, proposes marriage. The image 'Spread the corner of your garment' (v. 9) is used in much the same sense in Ezekiel 16:8 and Malachi 2:16. Moreover it echoes Boaz' own words in 2:12, where he wishes that Ruth may be richly blessed under the wings of the God of Israel. Just as God makes a covenant with his people to love and protect them, so Ruth asks Boaz to act (or rather to continue to act) in a similar way.

Boaz' reply shows that she has not misjudged the moment. He is certainly not offended by her forwardness but instead reveals that he is flattered rather than angry, and sees what she has done as evidence of further kindness (v. 10). What exactly is this 'kindness'? Surely, as an older man, he had feared that Ruth would inevitably be attracted by younger men and that he would have lost her. Moreover, he reveals that her words have fulfilled what he had not dared to hope. Again he praises Ruth. His description of her as a 'woman of noble character' (v. 11) recalls the narrator's description of him as a 'man of standing' (2:1).

Here we have a delicate and sensitive account of a couple taking the risk of declaring their love for each other, each nervous about the other's reaction. It is a beautifully human story and all who have experienced similar situations will empathize with it.

Scarcely have we rejoiced at the coming together of Ruth and Boaz when tension is heightened again. There is another relative of

Elimelech who stands in closer relationship than Boaz. Will Boaz lose Ruth after all? We, like Boaz, are going to have to wait to find out. He invokes Yahweh's name (v. 13) and swears a binding oath that he will fulfil his responsibilities.

Behind the story

To interpret this passage theologically, we have to respond to it imaginatively, but that does not mean engaging in unbridled imagination. Some commentators represent this kind of uncontrolled speculation. On the one hand, some see a scheming mother-in-law and a young girl flaunting herself to entrap a handsome and wealthy bachelor. On the other hand, some see a beautiful but penniless Ruth forcing herself to relate to an ageing and lecherous man who is nevertheless rich.

What we must do is to pick up hints from the narrative itself. While we do not know the emotions of the people concerned, we can take account of what the story has said of them. Ruth is now a devout believer in Israel's God (1:16), and her faith is well known, as shown by Boaz' remark that she has taken refuge under God's wings (2:12). Boaz' own faith is shown by his many references to Yahweh, whom he links with all his activities (2:4, 12; 3:10, 13). Both are shown to have the generosity and kindness that reflect Yahweh's own graciousness. This means that we expect their behaviour to flow from their commitment to the Lord and their witness to the faith and lifestyle associated with that commitment.

With that in mind, it is unthinkable that they should have done what they did without prayer. Although it is not mentioned explicitly, we know from the rest of scripture that faith in the Lord is impossible without prayer. This sense of an unmentioned dimension in the background of all that happens is even more a feature of Esther (see page 42 in this volume).

Theologically the story shows the guiding hand of Yahweh in events, discussions, initiatives and problems. Here is neither a fatalistic universe nor one marked by random chance. Rather, both in circumstances and in the human heart, God is working his purpose out.

REFLECTION

The more firmly we believe in God and his purposes, the more carefully will we think and act. By taking initiatives and risks, we will find that God is at work in our own lives and the lives of those around us.

9

Unfinished Business

Verses 14 and 15 are remarkable for their restraint. We have here a man and woman who have discovered their love for one another and who are at that most exciting, yet apprehensive of moments when the rest of their lives, with unknown possibilities and challenges, stretch out before them. The rest of the evening passes uneventfully but the tension is skilfully maintained. Now is not the time to go public, so Ruth leaves before dawn. The generosity of Boaz is again underlined: the grain he gives to Ruth is plentiful but not too onerous to carry.

The women bow out

The conversation between Ruth and Naomi that concludes this exciting chapter is brief but significant. Here both women speak for the last time in the book and bow off stage, although they are, of course, mentioned in chapter 4. Naomi's anxious enquiry sets the tone for the end of the chapter. Having advised action at the beginning of the episode, she now counsels caution. Naomi is called 'mother-in-law', a reminder that Ruth's status has not yet changed.

Ruth's reply is summarized (v. 16) but her final remarks emphasize Boaz' generous gift of food. This indicates that the emptiness theme of chapter 1 has now reached its conclusion. The famine is well and truly over and this is a sign that the other kind of emptiness, childlessness, will soon be over as well.

A number of important matters emerge from this brief exchange. The word 'wait' (v. 18) has the implication both of doing nothing else for the moment and of being patient. This chapter has concentrated on human resourcefulness and ingenuity but, now that all human steps have been taken, the outcome is in higher hands. The Hebrew phrase translated in the NIV as 'what happens' more literally reads 'how the matter falls out'. The metaphor is of a lot cast to find out which of two alternatives to take. We have already noticed the theological significance of similar phrases (see 2:3—'as it turned out') and here we find another veiled reference to the working of God behind the scenes.

Boaz spares no effort

Yet this outworking of Yahweh's plan will rely on Boaz relaxing no effort to see the matter brought to a satisfactory conclusion. He is a man of his word, who will not let either Naomi or Ruth down. He has already exemplified the compassion for widows and orphans that the prophets see as reflecting God's own character (see Isaiah 1:17; Zechariah 7:10); we are clearly approaching the end of the story.

Once again the author shows considerable literary skill. The episode closes on a note of great suspense. Chapters 1 and 2 ended with the author's comment but here the dialogue creates a cliffhanger. Though a first-time reader does not yet know it, we have heard for the last time from Naomi and Ruth, and yet what is to happen, particularly to Ruth, is eagerly anticipated.

Characterization has been cleverly developed through this chapter. Naomi cast off her bitterness and apathy and showed shrewdness and imagination as she devised the plan that set the events of that significant night in motion. Ruth showed both courage and sensitivity as she carried out her mother-in-law's very odd instructions. Boaz, who for the rest of the book is to take centre stage, has behaved with both dignity and kindness. We have already seen strong and developing emotions present, although never explicitly described.

Atmosphere is cleverly suggested. The darkness of the night, the loneliness of the place and the sense of something afoot are all sensitively and powerfully evoked. The technique here has been that of the close-up shot in the rather claustrophobic atmosphere of the threshing floor.

Plainly the climax of the whole story is approaching and we wait in suspense once again to see what the outcome will be.

REFLECTION

The life of faith is possible only because God himself is at work behind the scenes.

'Mr So-*and*-So' Enters & Exits

Events now move rapidly, and from the mystery and darkness of the threshing floor we move to the public arena of the town gate. This was a broad place where people congregated, and it served both as market and civic centre as well as being the centre for court cases to be heard. Here the closing scenes of the drama begin to unfold.

Will he, won't he?

Again there is a sense of a providential encounter. The text of verse 1 reads more literally 'and the kinsman-redeemer he had spoken about was passing by'. We have the sense (as in 2:3) that something momentous is about to happen.

It is fascinating to note that the kinsman's name is not given. We noticed back in chapter 1 that names were vital—even the hapless Mahlon and Kilion are named—and we shall see a similar emphasis at the end of this chapter. The NIV's phrase 'my friend' is reading too much into the text; the suggestion of 'Mr So-and-So' by some commentators probably catches the nuance exactly. This man has no real part in the story, or in the bigger story of 'great David and David's greater Son' (see comments on 4:19–22, p. 41).

We move now into the world of proper legal processes. Some have seen in the story a reference to 'levirate' law (Deuteronomy 25:7–9). *Levir* is Latin for 'brother-in-law'. This law was concerned to keep widows from marrying outside the family and to protect the family land. The events here in Ruth 4, however, do not reflect exactly the same situation, as the obligation is on the kinsman-redeemer (*go'el*) rather than the brother-in-law.

There are many obscurities in the following verses and interested readers should consult larger commentaries. It is important, though, to try to see as clearly as possible how Boaz brings this delicate matter to a satisfactory conclusion, for it is Boaz who is very much centre stage at this point. Once again, suspense builds up as we hold our breath and Mr So-and-So seems about to deprive Boaz of Ruth after all.

In verses 2–4, ten elders, presumably a quorum, are selected. Boaz here shows shrewdness by beginning his transaction with a piece of property rather than with Ruth, and thus diverting attention away from her. We have not hitherto heard of the piece of land belonging to Elimelech; our author still has the capacity to surprise us. Mr So-and-So agrees to redeem the land and, for a moment, we fear that Ruth and Boaz are not to be married after all.

Beginnings and endings

Boaz now introduces the case of Ruth, reminding us of both Naomi's early tragedy and Ruth's continuing status as a foreigner. Thus, as the story approaches its end, we are reminded of the situation from which it sprang. Mr So-and-So, in a revealing comment in verse 6, shows himself to be a contrast to Boaz. His own interests are the controlling factor in his life: 'I cannot redeem it because I might endanger my own estate.'

At this point the author, unusually, makes a comment to the reader (v. 7). This allows a pause for reflection and also bears very closely on the themes of the book, as well as linking it with other parts of the Old Testament. The giving of the sandal or shoe is a rather obscure custom but the symbolism is important. Removing the sandals (see Exodus 3:5; Joshua 5:15) was an acknowledgment of Yahweh's lordship, and to 'set foot' on land was a symbol of ownership (see Deuteronomy 1:36; Joshua 1:3). These passages are another means of linking Ruth's story with the overall story of the Bible. This is part of God's care and guidance of his people. Mr So-and-So's last words as he leaves the stage are 'Buy it yourself', which sound rather curt, and so he disappears as if he had never been.

PRAYER

Lord God, make us conscious of the significance of every decision
so that we do not miss our part in your great story. Amen.

GOD IS WORKING HIS PURPOSE OUT

Verses 9–10 fulfil a number of functions. Boaz completes the task by purchasing the property and speaking his last words in the book. What he says is precise and detailed and reminds us of the main themes of the story. The tragic trio of chapter 1 is mentioned again, as is, for the last time, Ruth's status as a foreigner and her widowhood. Now all this is caught up in both marriage and provision for the future. The final phrase, 'Today you are witnesses', echoes Joshua 24:22 and further links this story with the great story of Israel's possession of the land.

Ruth and the bigger story

It is verses 11 and 12, however, which confirm that this is far more than simply an account of an obscure legal transaction. The comprehensive blessing of verses 11–12 makes explicit the link between this story and the story of the nation; and Yahweh's blessing, often implicit, is now spelled out. Moreover, it is spelled out in such a way as to echo the main themes and emphases of the story. Rachel and Leah were the founding mothers of the nation and link Ruth specifically (as she has earlier been explicitly linked) with the story of Israel's ancestors.

Significantly, the story of Tamar in Genesis 38 is also evoked. Tamar was a Canaanite and, like Ruth, is to be part of Christ's own genealogy in Matthew 1. This is no legal transaction alone; this is the hand of Almighty God preserving the chosen line. Nor could anyone that day have imagined just how 'famous in Bethlehem' (v. 11) this line was to become.

Looking to the future

This is a rich and full chapter and three comments will help to draw together something of its impact. The first is that our impression of Boaz as a man of shrewdness, kindness and efficiency is underlined, and thus the action of chapters 2 and 3 is brought to a satisfactory conclusion. Boaz bows out, leaving us an impression of goodness and generosity, which are a reflection of Yahweh's own love.

Second, the story of Ruth is firmly tied to that of Israel and also shows us that foreigners who believe in Israel's God are accepted and welcomed into that story.

Third, we are pointed to the future. The emphasis is now to be on the children of the marriage of Boaz and Ruth, and how they are to affect the future not only of their immediate family but of Israel itself.

PRAYER

Lord God of eternity and of today, of the whole of history and this moment, we thank you that you are working out your purposes. Give us faith and vision to see our part and to do our tasks faithfully; through Jesus Christ, our Lord. Amen.

12

A Birth & a Blessing

Naomi blessed

As the story comes to a happy ending, the author deliberately echoes chapter 1. The emptiness of which Naomi spoke has now been swallowed up in blessing, and the future is secure. A brief verse (v. 13) swiftly encapsulates the events of almost a year, and Ruth's newborn infant is the centre of attention, along with Naomi.

This is rather unusual and calls for some comment. We do not have—as we might expect—any details of Ruth's and Boaz' life together. Indeed, some commentators argue that some kind of formal transaction is implied in these verses, whereby the child becomes Naomi's foster-son. Thus the expression in verse 16, 'cared for him', is understood as meaning that, for some undisclosed reason, the parents distanced themselves from their child's upbringing. As we shall see, this probably misinterprets the nuances of the text.

Yahweh's goodness

We shall understand better what is happening here if we examine two things. The first is the twofold reference to Yahweh's involvement in the situation. Verse 13 neatly summarizes the relationship between human activity and providence, which has been the main dynamic of this story. The love of Boaz and Ruth is sealed as they become united physically, yet it is Yahweh who causes their son to be born. This is more than nature taking its course; this son is a gift from God. Thus the human actors, very properly, are in the background.

The second reference to Yahweh's initiative is the identification of the child with the *go'el* (v. 14). So far, this has been the role of Boaz, and here an important point is being made. Whoever the human *go'el* may be at any given time, it is the Lord himself who is the true redeemer and thus the provider of all that is needed. This is a story of God's generosity and his care for his people.

The other thing to notice is that the focus on Naomi is the final undoing of her personal tragedy in 1:1–5, which launched the events of the whole book. Just as Yahweh has provided food, so now he provides an heir who will give both happiness and security to Naomi in her old age.

None of this means that Boaz and Ruth have inexplicably abandoned their responsibility for their child. We may assume, given what we know of their personalities, that they are fully involved. The interest of the author is elsewhere, however, and the focus is on the overruling of God in what had been tragic circumstance. This 'son' replaces the 'sons' lost in that other life in Moab.

Praise to God

The women in verses 14–15 act as a kind of chorus, rather like the 'daughters of Jerusalem' in the Song of Songs. When they announce the news of Obed's birth, they do so as an ascription of praise (v. 14), which probably sees the birth of the child as the culmination of God's overruling in the whole series of events from chapter 1 onwards. This is confirmed by the final reference to Ruth herself in verse 15. Ruth's love had reflected God's own, and her commitment and faithfulness had been one of the most significant factors in bringing this story to its happy conclusion. It is striking to hear the women say that this one woman is worth seven men (we shall see a similar favourable view of women in the Song of Songs).

The final vignette in the story comes when Naomi takes the child into her lap (v. 16). This is both a sign of her deep affection and also of the willingness of Boaz and Ruth to stand in the background to allow Naomi to savour the happiness of this moment to the full. Similarly, we should not make too much of the fact that the women (rather than the parents) named him Obed. The name is a shortened form of Obadiah, which means 'servant of Yahweh'—a further reminder of the story's centre of gravity. Who named this child is relatively unimportant; what matters is his part in God's overall purposes.

REFLECTION

Think of how you would tell the story of your life if you looked for evidence of God at work rather than focusing on the externals of the events and how people react to you.

TOWARDS *the* FUTURE

Names with a purpose

The story appears to have ended, yet, to our surprise, there is more. This final section is exactly the kind of writing that so often puts people off the Old Testament, as the charming and suspenseful narrative is followed by a list of names. This view is wholly mistaken, however. The apparently dull list powerfully underlines what the story is about, and we can see four key issues illustrated there.

The first is that this story of love and loyalty in Bethlehem, which might at first seem a moving but personal tale of two widows and their rescuer, is linked with Israel's national history. The child born here is the grandfather of the great King David himself. The homeless, landless girl from Moab has not only found a husband and a home-land but has also become the ancestor of Israel's royal house. Her story has been woven into God's own story. This is a major empha-sis in the book: our stories will become significant in so far as they become part of the great story.

Secondly, we now appreciate more fully the role of Yahweh in the various 'coincidences' already noted. The story began in the violent chaos of the period of the Judges, when 'everyone did as he saw fit' (Judges 21:25). It ends by pointing to the emergence of the great national leader who was to be the model for all later kings. God, in spite of appearances, was in control.

Thirdly, we see (as in all the Bible's genealogies) the importance of ordinary people as well as the great names. We begin with Perez, whose birth to Tamar, Judah's daughter, is recorded in Genesis 38:29. Then follows a list of people about whom virtually nothing is known. An exception is Nahshon, brother-in-law of Aaron (Exodus 6:23), who was selected as the tribal leader of Judah (Numbers 1:7). Whether well-known or obscure, though, these people were all vital links in the chain that was to lead to David himself. We should never underestimate the importance of the unsung lives that God weaves into his purposes.

David announced

Fourthly, and most importantly, we are given a glimpse into the divine preservation of the line of David and of his rise to prominence, but we can go further still. This genealogy anticipates the one set out in Matthew 1. There, Ruth takes her place along with other women who were outsiders but who were nevertheless significant not only for David but for 'great David's greater son'. Tamar, Rahab, Ruth and Bathsheba were significant figures not only for the line of David but for Jesus himself. They show the generosity of God spilling out beyond national boundaries and embracing the whole world.

The book of Ruth is not simply a charming story from a vanished world, although of course, at face value, it is that. It is not simply a cleverly crafted narrative with a compelling plot, rounded characters and a convincing setting, although it is that too. It is not simply a fascinating study of human activity and initiative. It is part of the great story of God the lover, who cares for and guides his people, who searches for and welcomes the outsider and who works out his purposes of love through seeming coincidences.

MEDITATION

Probably the best comment on the book of Ruth is found in Paul's words in 1 Corinthians 13:13: 'And now these three remain: faith, hope and love. But the greatest of these is love.'

14   ESTHER

INTRODUCTORY ISSUES

Readers who expect the Bible to be filled with improving stories are in for a rude shock when they open the Old Testament. Nowhere is this more marked than in the book of Esther. Here is a book about attempted ethnic cleansing, extravagant ostentation, greed, power politics and a very ambiguous set of characters. Worse than that, the name of God is not mentioned and there is no allusion to the scriptures, to prayer, sacrifice or any of the normal expressions of Israel's faith. At first sight it is not easy to see why the book is in the Bible at all. Yet, as we shall see, it is astonishingly relevant to the contemporary world, as well as being beautifully written. The issues raised above will be addressed throughout the commentary, but for our first study we shall look at some introductory questions.

When was it written?

The book shows great familiarity with Persian court life and lifestyle as these are known from other sources. Its setting is the early decades of the fifth century BC (around 485–465BC) and it takes place in the city of Susa, where the royals had a winter palace. Some have suggested Mordecai as the author (see 9:20, 32), and some of the content probably comes from the royal annals (for example, 6:1; 10:2). Certainty is impossible but if the history in the book is authentic (the view taken in this commentary), a date in the Persian period is likely.

What kind of book is it?

Some recent studies have seen the book of Esther as a kind of embryonic novel with perhaps a few historical allusions. Some have seen it as a legend to explain the origin of the festival of Purim, which is not mentioned in the Torah. Nothing in the story is impossible or even improbable, however, and the background accords with what we know of ancient Persian life and culture. I believe that what we have here is history, but, as with other Old Testament history, it is presented not only to inform but to instruct, enlighten and lead to change. At the same time, we shall have to listen carefully for the clues that do not lie on the surface.

What issues are raised?

Five main themes can be identified.

- The hiddenness of God: Since God is not mentioned, we must read this book with the eyes of faith. Thus it is particularly relevant for those living in a world where he appears to be absent and his influence non-existent.

- Providence and human responsibility: We saw how this was a major theme in Ruth. The key passage here in Esther is 4:12–14 (see pp. 64–65).

- Diaspora: This term, often translated 'dispersion' (see, for example, 1 Peter 1:1, RSV) raises questions about whether there is a Jewish faith and identity beyond Jerusalem. In the story, some 60 years have passed since the end of the exile and a substantial part of the Jewish community has yet to return to their homeland.

- Gender issues: Esther has attracted attention from feminist scholars, and much of its material, especially in chapters 1 and 2, has been examined from that perspective.

- Links with the rest of scripture: An important key for the interpretation of Esther is links with other parts of the Bible, in particular the Joseph and Daniel stories, as well as part of Exodus and the death of John the Baptist.

PRAYER

*God our Father, help us to be open to all that your word says,
even when it speaks in strange and unfamiliar ways. Amen.*

15 ESTHER 1:1-9

The KING IN ALL HIS GLORY

The author sets out clearly the personalities and setting and draws the reader into the world of the story. 'This is what happened' (v. 1) is the usual formula for introducing a historical narrative.

First we are introduced to the person who we imagine will be the principal character in the story. Xerxes (called Ahasuerus in some translations) reigned from 486 to 465BC. His empire was immense, stretching from, in contemporary terms, Pakistan to northern Sudan. Already we are given the impression of overwhelming power. The scene is Susa, where the royal court spent the winter. This city is also mentioned in Daniel 8:2 as the scene of Daniel's vision of the ram and the male goat, which, ironically, focuses on the destruction of the Persian empire.

The time is 'the third year of his reign' (v. 3). We know that in that year a great council was held to discuss a military operation against Greece. Our author says nothing of this, however, and concentrates on the accompanying banquet, with its inordinate length of 180 days. This banquet doubtless had an important political purpose (v. 4). Probably the 'nobles and officials' were being flattered and wined and dined to secure their loyalty. The emphasis is on showing off the king's wealth, luxury and power. All is calculated to impress, overawe and probably intimidate.

Boundless extravagance

Everything here is in technicolour; it is extravagant and overwhelming. Indeed, we may wonder what nourishment we can find in these verses. In fact, our author is subtly suggesting the character of king and court and providing a perspective for assessing characters and interpreting events as they unfold.

The description of the banquet confines itself to the ostentatious luxury of its setting. Herodotus, the Greek historian, describes how, more than a century later, even Alexander the Great was amazed at the incredible wealth of the palace at Susa. No overt comment is made but warning bells ring. This wealth and apparent power are to prove illusory. Thus, early in the story, we have a motif running through: the disparity of appearance and reality.

The other item emphasized is the extravagant liberality of the wine (v. 8). The Bible does not condemn wine; indeed it sees it as one of God's good gifts (see Psalm 104:15: 'wine that gladdens the human heart'). It condemns excess, however, and in Daniel 5 we have another example of extravagant wine-drinking at Belshazzar's feast, with its disastrous consequences.

Meanwhile, Queen Vashti holds a parallel banquet for the women (v. 9). The very absence of comment about inordinate luxury and excessive drinking suggests that our author is already presenting Vashti in a more favourable light.

We are not yet launched into the story, and it is worth pausing to reflect briefly on what the author has done in the introductory scene setting. Three factors call for comment.

The first is the storyteller's art. The author neither condemns Xerxes nor commends Vashti. He does not moralize on ostentation or the evils of drinking to excess, but simply paints a word-picture of power, luxury and drinking that are all larger than life. We are left with an uneasy feeling and a sense of foreboding. How long can this state of affairs continue?

The second is the theme, already noticed, of appearance and reality. The description in verses 4–6 is quite unusual in biblical narrative. Similar passages about colour and materials occur in the descriptions of the tent in the desert (Exodus 25—28) and of the temple (1 Kings 7; 2 Chronicles 3—4). There the colour and beauty were for the glory of God; here they are for the glory of Xerxes. Indeed, in verse 4 that very phrase is used: 'the... glory of his majesty'. Here is a man who thinks of himself as a god. It is striking also that in Esther there is no mention of pagan gods, any more than of the true God. Rather, the reality behind idolatry is exposed, because idolatry is at the root of worship of self.

Third, suspense and excitement are created. The opening words, 'This is what happened', arouse expectations of something significant. So far we have seen only the backdrop. We wait eagerly for the main story to begin.

REFLECTION

It is vital to look at the worldly power and splendour from the perspective of faith and not to be overawed by appearances.

The KING HUMILIATED

Xerxes' command to Vashti is of a piece with what we have already come to expect of him. If he has already displayed 'the vast wealth of his kingdom and the splendour and glory of his majesty' (1:4), he now wants to show off his queen, demonstrating that he regards her simply as one of his possessions (v. 11).

Almost immediately the king's drunken megalomania crashes into the buffers. Vashti simply refuses to come. The great king is reduced to fuming impotence, and his anger—like all else about him—is extravagant and overstated: 'the king became furious and burned with anger' (v. 12).

Biting irony

The irony continues as, with heavy-handed officialdom, he summons the privy council. Again we have echoes of Daniel. These 'wise men who understood the times' (v. 13) are people like the astrologers and diviners on whom Nebuchadnezzar and Belshazzar relied (Daniel 2:2; 5:7). We cannot fail to notice that it requires a solemn conclave to sort out the king's marital problems, with a decision that any male chauvinist could have dreamed up instantly. This is a man for whom relationships are simply another form of power politics.

Memucan, the spokesman for the group, widens the incident and uses it to make a general statement about the roles of husbands and wives (vv. 16–18). The extravagance of his reaction shows not power but nervousness. The juggernaut of irrevocable law is to be employed not only against Vashti but against every wife 'throughout all his vast realm' (v. 20). Irrevocable law also features in Daniel, in the famous story of the lions' den (Daniel 6:8, 12, 15), and is to appear again in this story when Haman tries to use it to destroy the Jews. This group of men is greedy to retain power and they want to ensure that no one can stand in their way.

We shall miss much of the thrust of the story if we miss the humour. We must not take the characters as seriously as they take themselves. The next ironic note is that Vashti 'is never again to enter the presence of King Xerxes' (v. 19). Since this is almost certainly what she wants, it is a meaningless punishment.

Moreover, by issuing the decree, the king only succeeds in advertising his own domestic failure in the widest possible way. Memucan is a rather inept spin-doctor. Power blinds the council to reality. Ironically, they take steps that ensure what they wish to prevent: 'the queen's conduct will become known to all the women, and so they will despise their husbands' (v. 17).

The bigger picture

At the end of the chapter another theme is introduced: the multi-national, multi-lingual nature of Persian society (v. 22). This echoes an important note in the biblical canon as a whole. In Genesis 11:7–9, after the building of the tower of Babel, human languages are confused. Then Abraham is called by God, so that all nations will be blessed (Genesis 12:3). On the day of Pentecost, everyone hears the gospel in their own language (Acts 2:7–11). Finally, a crowd 'from every nation, tribe, people and language' stand before God and the Lamb (Revelation 7:9). Xerxes may think he is in control, but his vast and transient power is only part of the story.

The scene has been set and some of the characters introduced. We can observe already that human power is vast and imposing and has the appearance of stability. The reality is that not only do all regimes come to an end but that, even at their height, they are constrained by all kinds of hidden influences. Here we see the interplay of sexual and national politics. Power is closely linked to the strengths and weaknesses of the individuals who exercise it.

We also note that this book is part of the scriptures. We shall continue to see how other key parts of the Old Testament are echoed at critical moments in the story of Esther.

MEDITATION

To help us to put the book of Esther in its widest context, it would be good to meditate on these words:

Why do nations conspire and the peoples plot in vain? The kings of the earth take their stand and the rulers gather together against the Lord and against his Anointed One. 'Let us break their chains,' they say, 'and throw off their fetters.' The One enthroned in heaven laughs; the Lord scoffs at them.

Psalm 2:1–4

17

A BEAUTY CONTEST

In the manner of stories, we now jump three years (see 2:16)—years when Xerxes was fighting a losing war with Greece. This is a chapter full of ambiguities and cross-currents, with the king still attempting to manipulate people and events and yet in reality becoming increasingly marginalized. In a sense, this is still part of the scene-setting before the action properly begins in chapter 3, and we have still to meet some of the main characters. Four main movements make up this chapter, each making its own contribution to the narrative. Here in this first movement, three themes are prominent.

Writing Vashti out of the story

In recent years, the word 'airbrushing' has become common in political discourse. The term refers to the rewriting of history that always happens in political parties and other institutions when new people come to prominence. Older figures, whose faces no longer fit, fall victim to a kind of collective amnesia among the incoming élite. This is what is happening to Vashti here. The author of Ecclesiastes is well aware of this phenomenon: 'There is no remembrance of people of old' (1:11; see comment, p. 89). Here it is another example of Xerxes' petulance and smouldering anger.

A despicable scheme

Xerxes continues his policy of seeing women simply as possessions to be used for his own pleasure (v. 4). Not that this shows simply an anti-female attitude, however: Herodotus tells us that five hundred boys were castrated each year to serve as eunuchs in the Persian court. The reality is that when people take to themselves godlike powers, they treat other human beings merely in accordance with their personal whims.

This shows how important it is for human power to be subject to checks and balances. Today Xerxes would be indicted for child abuse (the girls would probably have been in their early teens), serial rape and serious assault. After a night of anxious and probably tearful suspense, the girls would be confined to the harem for the rest of their lives. 'Under the care of Hegai, the king's eunuch' (v. 3) is surely ironic and conceals a world of unhappiness.

The Bible never shrinks from exposing the uglier side of human nature and, indeed, underlines it to show both how serious is human sin and how wonderful is the grace of God (see, for example, Romans 1:18–32). We do well to see what human beings (including ourselves) are capable of when we abandon our divinely given role as creatures and set ourselves up as gods in our own universe. Few, if any, readers of these pages will have the power of Xerxes, but we are all in danger, in our own worlds, of treating others as disposable commodities for our own ends.

A hidden hand

'This advice appealed to the king, and he followed it' (v. 4). Xerxes, as we have seen, appears to be incapable of doing anything without advice, and such advice always comes to him from sycophants who say only what they are sure will please him. Again, he thinks he is in control, but the very scheme he initiates will bring into his life someone who is to be instrumental in undoing all he stands for.

A good commentary on the story of Xerxes would be Proverbs 21:1: 'The king's heart is in the hand of the Lord; he directs it like a watercourse wherever he pleases.' God uses everything—Xerxes' own instability, the flattery of the courtiers, human greed and cruelty—to work out his purposes in the godless Persian empire. A hidden hand is at work and events are to take many unexpected turns.

Here again we have the theme of appearance and reality. Looks are to be high on the agenda when the king makes his choice. The combination of the phrases 'beautiful girls' and 'let beauty treatments be given to them' (v. 3) shows that we are indeed in the world of beauty contests.

REFLECTION

*The Bible will not allow us to hide away from the unpleasant
realities of human nature—not so that we can wallow in them but
to show us how we need God's grace to remake our lives.*

The PLAYERS ARRIVE

At this point, two new characters are introduced who will alter the situation profoundly.

A man with a past

Mordecai is introduced in a way that links him not only with the recent past of his people but with more distant times (v. 5). He was a descendant of Kish, who had been taken into exile in 597BC, but there is more. A much earlier Kish, also a Benjaminite, was the father of King Saul and perhaps a more remote ancestor of Mordecai. This is a man whose history is rooted in that of his people, and we are now to see another significant series of events in the history of those people.

His name also includes an allusion to Marduk the Babylonian god, and this is a reminder of Daniel 1, where Daniel and his friends are given names that contain allusions to pagan deities. Thus, in a sense, Mordecai's name dramatizes the main issue of the book, which is how to remain faithful to God in a pagan environment. Also in verse 5, he is called a 'Jew' (see also 6:10; 8:7; 9:29, 31; 10:3), which reminds us of the powerful racist current present in the story.

A question that obviously arises is whether Mordecai was right to put Esther into such a compromising situation, where she is compelled to conceal her faith (v. 10). Once again, the author does not comment. Perhaps we are raising the wrong question. The ancient author is less interested in the motives of the characters and more in the way that God is using them to protect his people and fulfil his purposes. The fact that God uses people in this way is not an indication of their godliness—a striking example being his use of the pagan emperor Cyrus to reverse the exile and allow God's people to return to their own land: 'This is what the Lord says to his anointed, to Cyrus, whose right hand I take hold of to subdue nations before him' (Isaiah 45:1).

A woman with a future

When Esther is introduced, two things are emphasized: she is an orphan and she is beautiful (v. 7). She also has a Hebrew name:

Hadassah, which means 'myrtle'. Esther may be the Hebrew form of 'Ishtar', a powerful Babylonian goddess of love and war. Here again are hints of what is to come, for love and war are to be at the heart of the unfolding story.

Nothing is said about Esther's feelings as she is taken into the king's harem. Harems could be places of fear and humiliation, yet this is not Esther's experience, with special treatment laid on in 'the best place in the harem' (v. 9). Moreover, Mordecai makes it his business to keep an eye on her and ensure that all is well (v. 11).

It is never easy to combine faithfulness to God with a positive and constructive engagement to the world. A useful comment on this is Romans 12:2, 'Do not conform any longer to the pattern of this world, but be transformed by the renewing of your mind', but knowing how to do it is not easy. There are huge areas of ambiguity where Christians have difficult and complex choices to make.

It is very difficult to be a faithful Christian in high office, because of pressures and temptations about which most of us know nothing. Similarly, the fields of medical ethics, business and journalism present many situations that do not always fit easily into a Christian lifestyle.

We need to bear in mind three issues. The first is that we require great wisdom and discernment to know how to act in complex situations. Nor can we judge the motives and pressures on those who act differently in situations other than our own.

Second, we must pray for people in government and other areas of importance in national life, such as the media. It is vital that Christians in such positions have the prayerful support of fellow Christians. This is an area often neglected.

Third—and this is an important principle for interpreting biblical narrative—the characters in Esther are not held up to us as examples to follow. Rather, this is part of God's story; he is working through people whose motives are unknown and whose actions are often dubious. In this licentious, sinister and extravagant Persian court, God is working his purpose out.

PRAYER

God our Father, we pray for Christian people in situations of inter-national, national and local leadership. We ask that they may be faithful to you and that you will raise up many others to join them. We pray in the name of Jesus Christ our Lord. Amen.

GOD *at* WORK EVEN HERE

This section reminds us of the Persian court (1:5–9) and the extravagance that marks its life.

Excess in all things

Extravagance is the key note of this passage; everything is inflated. The length of time for the beautifying and make-up process is inordinate (v. 12). Spices and oils were a major part of the economy of rich and powerful nations in the ancient world, and here they are used with reckless abandon. Everything seems designed to create an atmosphere of sensuality and indulgence—'anything she wanted' (v. 13)—but it is accompanied by heartlessness and a cavalier disregard for human sensitivity. The unsuccessful girls (the overwhelming majority) were returned to the harem (v. 14). Certainly they would live a life of luxury, but it would be grim and uncertain and they would never see their families again.

Esther's turn

The passage means what it says (v. 17): Esther presumably outperformed the others in bed and dazzled the king. The word 'marriage' is not mentioned, but presumably 'made her queen' (v. 17) implies it. This is the very time when marriage with Gentiles had become a burning issue with the Jewish community back home (see Ezra 9:12; 10:10–17). Yet this Jewish girl experiences the sensual luxury of a harem, has sex with and marries a pagan monarch and becomes queen of a godless empire.

What was her motivation and what did she believe she was doing? Was she filled with fear and loathing and did it only because it would help her people? There is no hint of that in the text, and, in any case, there is no threat to her people at this moment. Was she flattered and swept off her feet, thinking it was the best thing that had ever happened to her? Again, the text is silent. There is simply no comment from the narrator on the violations of the Torah seen here.

This means that the intention cannot possibly be an exemplary one. How different it all is from Joseph in Egypt resisting the advances of Potiphar's wife (Genesis 39). What could the example be? What would you say to your teenage daughter as she reads this story?

What is it all about?

A surface reading would lead to a view of life in which the end justifies the means. Is a teenager to assume from the story that it is good to be as seductive as possible to powerful men? The author plainly does not in any sense intend to hold up Esther here as a virtuous woman, obedient to God's law, but neither does he condemn her. We do not read, 'What Esther did displeased the Lord' (compare 2 Samuel 11:27). What, then, are we to make of it?

We must first see Esther as caught up in a complex and ambiguous situation. Moreover, she is in this situation as a result of the advice of her guardian Mordecai, whose judgment she trusted. Ruth 3 shows, in a much less lurid and melodramatic way, something of the same complexities (see commentary on that chapter, pp. 28–31). Life is rarely simple in this fallen world, and easy answers are not always possible. Often we have to choose between various unsatisfactory alternatives.

This further bears on the problem of guidance (as does Ruth 3). In many situations we cannot make simplistic judgments, nor should others try to make them for us. It may often feel as if God has left us without guidance.

When we are in such situations, though, where whatever choice we make seems unsatisfactory, we can take courage that God is working behind the scenes. Even if we make the wrong decisions, God can use them in his larger plan. We have no way of knowing how Esther looked back on this episode. What we do know is that God used her to fulfil his purposes and save his people.

REFLECTION

Look back on your past experiences and consider how God has used them in bringing you to where you are today. Remember too that he is not finished with you, and that current events will also be woven into his pattern for your life.

Uneasy Lies *the* Head...

From the world of sexual politics, we return to that of state politics and to the first of many 'coincidences' in the book. The king's 'gate' (v. 19) was not simply an entrance but a large area where business was transacted and justice administered (see, for example, Deuteronomy 17:5, 8). The fact that what happens here is intimately linked to the previous scene, in spite of appearances, is shown by the reference to Esther continuing to follow Mordecai's instructions (v. 20). Esther will not abandon her heritage.

Another significant feature of this episode of a plot to assassinate Xerxes is weakness behind the apparently invincible regime. How Mordecai finds out about the plot is unknown, but he acts promptly, telling Queen Esther (as she is called in verse 22), and the plotters are summarily executed. There is a 'documentary' feel to this little section, and later we find that it is an extract from the chronicles of Xerxes' reign (v. 23; 6:1–2). Moreover, the plotting here foreshadows that of chapter 6.

Unfolding events

We will focus on two issues here. The first is the place of 'coincidence'. In Ruth 2:3 (see commentary, p. 23) attention is drawn to an apparently accidental event by using the phrase 'as it turned out'. Here, Mordecai happens to be at the gate when Bigthana and Teresh are plotting to assassinate the king.

Mordecai's presence at the gate was due to an official position he held, as indicated by the phrase 'sitting at the king's gate' (v. 19). However, since the reference to Mordecai is instantly followed by a mention of Esther, the author is plainly suggesting that he is also very concerned for her continuing welfare. Throughout scripture, important events often happen when people are pursuing routine work. Moses was tending sheep when God appeared to him (Exodus 3); young Samuel had carried out routine duties and was lying down to sleep when the Lord called him (1 Samuel 3); supremely, it was to the shepherds guarding their flocks that the angels brought the message of the birth of the Saviour (Luke 2). This does not mean that striking revelations and significant events will happen every day of our lives. Rather, it suggests that we do not know which of the multitude of apparently insignificant events will change our lives and those of others.

The book of Esther is deeply concerned with the mysterious working of God behind and in all the chaotic and unpredictable events of our lives. A former British Prime Minister, Harold Macmillan, was once asked what the most difficult thing was about the job. He replied, 'Events, dear boy, events.' When we feel at the mercy of events, it is an immense strength to know that all of the 'changes and chances of this fleeting life' are part of God's overall plan. Like the events in Esther, they seem fragmentary and disconnected, but they are part of the big story that God has planned and will complete.

Acting in character

The second issue is revealed in the phrase in verse 22: when Esther reports the incident to the king, she does so 'giving credit to Mordecai'. We have already seen in verse 20 that she still gives Mordecai loyalty, affection and respect. Here we see that her new position has not gone to her head—and this realization should make us hesitate to be too condemnatory about her actions earlier in the chapter. Nothing would have been easier for her than to have told the story in such a way as to reflect credit on herself.

Here our author is suggesting an important principle. While Esther and the other characters in the book are not presented as normal examples for us to follow, little details like this suggest that character is important. Just as Mordecai learned of the plot as he carried out his normal duties, so Esther acted generously, and God uses both factors to work out his purposes. We are not puppets; our attitudes and actions matter. Likewise we hear no complaints from Mordecai when no recognition comes for his service to the king.

Chapter 2 ends with the main lines of the plot laid down and most of the characters in place. Whatever may be the complexities of the situation and the ambivalence of the characters, we cannot but admire the remarkable resilience and attractiveness of Esther and the courage and perseverance of Mordecai. Enormous responsibilities are to rest on the shoulders of these two as the story unfolds.

PRAYER

Lord God help us to be faithful in our daily lives, diligent in our work and open to your guiding through all the changes of our lives.

ENTER *the* VILLAIN

Xerxes now, and not for the first time, displays his lack of judgment. Whatever this new character Haman may have done, the honours given to him are excessive, and remind us of the ostentation of chapter 1.

The old enemy

Although Haman is a new character, the description of him as 'the Agagite' is significant and ominous. Agag was king of the Amalekites, one of Israel's traditional enemies at the time of King Saul (1 Samuel 15). Previously, they had attacked the Israelites as they journeyed through the desert (Exodus 17). Saul failed to exterminate them as commanded by Samuel, and they remained as a thorn in the flesh to the Israelites. The author is indicating that here we have a deadly enemy of the Jewish nation, whose influence on their destiny is likely to be malign.

The introduction of Haman does a number of things. It reminds us of the ostentation and sycophancy of the court; it alerts the reader to a possible danger to Mordecai and his people; and it reminds us of the impulsive and irrational nature of Xerxes' actions. Thus, in the narrator's skilful way, suspense is built up and new possibilities emerge.

Taking a stand

We are not told why Mordecai would not bow to Haman (v. 2). It was certainly not out of disrespect for Xerxes, to whom he had just proved his loyalty. However, it is likely that he recognized Haman as an inveterate enemy as well as someone bristling with self-importance and unworthy of such an honour. Thus he resisted continuous pressure from the royal officials to bow.

We may compare Mordecai's action with Daniel's three friends' refusal to bow to Nebuchadnezzar's image (Daniel 3) and Daniel's own refusal to stop praying at the king's command (Daniel 6). Although God is not mentioned in Esther, Mordecai would not have feared any earthly potentate, because his God, in the words of Daniel, 'changes times and seasons; he sets up kings and deposes them' (Daniel 2:21).

Every age needs people of integrity who cannot be bought and who will stand up for what is right, even when it is difficult and dangerous. Just how dangerous Mordecai's stand was, we are about to see.

Racism rears its head

Haman has already been told that Mordecai is a Jew (v. 5) and now sees the opportunity to exterminate the whole nation. Here Haman is revealed in his true colours as a would-be initiator of what is now called genocide. Like Hitler, Pol Pot and the extremists in 1994 in Rwanda, he is determined to exterminate a whole people. Such hatred is megalomania—the ultimate idolatry of a man who thinks he is God.

REFLECTION

There will be often be circumstances in which integrity requires us to take a stand, although it will be inconvenient and perhaps dangerous. Pray that, when such times come, we will have the God-given courage to do what is necessary.

THE DIE IS CAST

This section begins with a time note: 'the twelfth year of King Xerxes' (v. 7). Five years have now passed since Esther became queen (2:16–17). During this time Mordecai has detected the conspiracy against Xerxes (3:1–5) and Haman has risen to power.

The casting of lots

In spite of his overweening arrogance and great power, Haman is superstitious. Those around him cast lots to discover what will be the best time for the evil plan against the Jews to proceed. Thus they cast a *pur*—a kind of dice or lot. *Pur* is to be significant later in giving its name to the festival of Purim. The lot falls on the 13th day on the twelfth month (vv. 7, 13). Surely here we see the workings of chance and a random universe, yet even this is under the control of God. Proverbs 16:33 says, 'The lot is cast into the lap, but its every decision is from the Lord.' In other words, when blind chance seems most utterly dominant, even there God is in control of events and can overrule.

This is not to advocate casting lots as a way of making decisions, but we see that there are no circumstances that God cannot control. More and more, as the story unfolds, we are to see the workings of God and his role in events as they unfold.

There is a further fascinating detail. The death edict is issued on the 13th day of the first month, nearly a year before it is to be carried out (vv. 12–13). Immediately the stakes are raised. The 13th of the first month was the eve of the Passover (see Exodus 12:18; Leviticus 23:5; Numbers 28:16). On that day, the God of Israel had rescued his people: could he do it again? Haman thinks he is in charge of events but he is playing with fire.

The manipulation of the truth

An important theme introduced in chapter 1 was the mismatch between appearance and reality. In chapter 3, Haman's denunciation of the Jews to the king is a mixture of truths, half-truths and lies (v. 8). The reference to the 'certain people' scattered throughout the empire is true enough, but the fact that they follow different customs is no more than would be expected in such a large and diverse empire. The accusation that they 'do not obey the king's laws' (v. 8) is a lie: Mordecai and Esther are the only Jews we have so far met in the book, and they have been conspicuously loyal. Haman appeals to the king's self-interest: suspicious and paranoid as Xerxes is, this would be a powerful motive. He also appeals to the king's greed (v. 9): the royal treasury would have been severely depleted not only by Xerxes' extravagance but by his costly wars with Greece.

Xerxes does not come out well from this episode. He bears all the marks of a man surrounded by sycophants on whom he has come to rely for his view of the world. He does not ask Haman to produce evidence; he does not even enquire who the 'certain people' are. Xerxes gives Haman *carte blanche*, and then characteristically sits down to have a drinking session with him, showing total lack of concern for human life (v. 15).

Haman may be evil and amoral but he is certainly thorough. Every part of the empire is to be covered and the whole machinery of the state is set in motion to ensure that the Jews are annihilated and their possessions plundered (v. 13). The effect on the Jewish community is stunned bewilderment (v. 15), in total contrast to the chilling evil of Haman and the cavalier shrugs of Xerxes.

Here we see that there are forces bent on destroying God's cause in the world and thwarting God's purposes. Thus it was for the early Christians in the Roman empire when they refused to give the name 'Lord' to anyone except Jesus Christ. Thus it still is in some countries today, where the state acts like God and leaders behave with a megalomaniac ambition and disregard for life. Just as God is not mentioned in the book of Esther, neither is Satan, but there is a malign force at work in the Persian state (see also Daniel 10:13), trying to destroy the Jews and thus ultimately prevent the Messiah from being born. A later tyrant tried to kill him after his birth (Matthew 2), and a still later one succeeded in killing him, only to find that not even death could thwart God's purposes.

PRAYER

Lord God, we thank you that no power in heaven or earth can ultimately thwart your purposes. Give us faith and vision to see that, even in perplexing and dangerous times. Amen.

CRYING *without* RELIEF

For the moment, exalted thoughts of God's overall purpose seem remote and unreal. Mordecai hears the news with great distress, which displays itself in the visible signs of tearing clothes, wearing sackcloth and ashes, and loud weeping (v. 3).

The wider issues

This is far more than the grief of an individual, however; the entire Jewish nation was involved—'in every province' (v. 3)—which would include the group of former exiles who had returned to their homeland. Huge questions arise. Is God absent, not just in the text, but from the whole situation? What about his control of history? Has he raised up Cyrus to reverse the exile, only for that concession to be undone by Haman? The fickleness of human protection now is cruelly obvious. Mordecai seems excluded from the seat of power: 'he went only as far as the king's gate' (v. 2).

All this is a powerful reminder of the need for faith. Much of the time, God will seem to be absent, and we will often experience circumstances that appear to call in question his very existence. Then, we do not show faith by a kind of bravado but rather by facing our humanity and vulnerability.

The place of fasting

The vulnerability and dependence of the Jews are expressed here by fasting (v. 3). A lot of the story, as we have already seen, is marked by feasting. This feasting is on a colossal scale and evokes in the reader a sense of waste and extravagance. It is worth reflecting a little, therefore, on the significance of fasting. It would certainly have been accompanied by prayer. Although that is not specifically mentioned here, in the book of Daniel the connection is underlined. Chapters 8—12 of that book show Daniel fasting and praying as he contemplates the great things God is doing to bring about the end of the exile. Similarly, Ezra calls for a fast (8:21) and Nehemiah fasts and prays (1:4).

Thus we may reasonably assume that the prayer of Mordecai and the Jewish people was continual and urgent as the reality of the danger sank in. Some commentators have argued that since praying is not explicitly mentioned, it cannot have taken place. In a similar passage, however, Joel (2:12–14) mentions the same three verbs— 'fasting, weeping and mourning'. This is in the context of a call to repentance, yet Joel does not mention the word 'prayer'.

Prayer and fasting are an acknowledgment that we have reached the end of our resources. Social customs of the time, such as tearing clothes and the use of sackcloth and ashes, should not blind us to the enduring significance of the issues. These physical actions are not so much significant in themselves as outward signs of inward emotions and trauma. Perhaps in our 'cooler' and more laid-back culture, we have overlooked the powerful symbolism of such behaviour. What is at stake is how seriously we engage with God.

Another issue is the relationship of prayer and fasting to God's overall purpose. Fasting is not magic; nor indeed is prayer. Nor must we suppose that, if these actions are not present, God cannot and does not work. Rather, the fact that God's people are doing these things is a sign that God is already working.

REFLECTION

Fasting is not compulsory, yet we probably need to consider more often whether there are times when it would be appropriate.

CAN ESTHER HELP?

Here, as in the previous study, we see the cross-currents of the story. While Haman appears to have constant access to the king, it seems that Esther does not. Thirty days have passed since Xerxes last requested to see her. The fear that she would now be treated like Vashti would make her extremely vulnerable. She knows that her husband is not to be trusted, and she fears the world of power politics. As we have already seen, the king was a man of extreme mood swings (v. 11) and is apparently now completely under Haman's influence.

Esther's identity crisis

In the world of the court, it was probably all too easy to be shielded from ordinary concerns, but now Esther faces a moment of decision as Mordecai's messenger shows her a copy of the edict of annihilation (v. 8). Some commentators have pointed out that Esther is the only person in the story with two names: her Hebrew name, Hadassah, and her Persian name, Esther. As in the case of Daniel, who was called Belteshazzar by his Babylonian captors (Daniel 1:7), these names represent the two worlds in which Esther lives: when these worlds clash, difficult and dangerous decisions have to be made. Few of us will be in such a predicament as Esther, yet each of us faces moments of decision, and the choices we make are crucial for the future course of our lives. There is an ambiguity in the phrase 'her people' (v. 8). Is this allegiance what Esther in her heart feels, or is it what Mordecai wants her to feel?

Esther's initiative

After hearing of Mordecai's mourning, Esther does not simply wait and hope for the best. She sends Hathach, one of her attendants, to find out what is happening (v. 5). He discovers the whole sordid truth, including how much Haman has offered the king. Esther also sends a message to Mordecai, informing him of the danger of approaching the king (v. 11). All of this adds to the human interest of the story. These people are like us, with the same fears and doubts and the same need for safety and security. Like us, they lived in a world of uncertainty and did not know what the outcome of their decisions and actions would be. It is important as we read biblical narrative to empathize with the characters and to enter their stories. If we fail to do so, we are in danger of seeing only the surface of the story and missing the underlying significance. Esther faced a real dilemma. She was Persian royalty but also one of a people destined for annihilation by the Persian royal laws. Should she be loyal to Mordecai or to Xerxes?

Living in a pagan world

We have commented on the many ambiguities of this story and the mixed characters of the people involved. It has not been a simple matter of seeing clearly who or what is right or wrong. Matters are now approaching a crisis, though. Up to this point, events seem to have been simply the result of the whims of some of the leading characters, with little sense of any divine overruling or direction. Up to now, Esther has been passive, not initiating any action, but now she has to take responsibility for her future and that of others.

Some biblical stories, such as those of Daniel or Joseph, show very plainly how to live in a pagan world. Here the issues are much more indirect, and yet, as the story unfolds, no less powerful and significant. The Daniel and Joseph stories specifically mention God and prayer, and show how these characters' lives were shaped by their relationship with God. In the case of Daniel, numerous references to the Torah underline his commitment to a godly lifestyle. Here in Esther, as already noted, there is ambiguity and a lack of direct reference to God and the Torah.

PRAYER

Lord, help us in the confusion of our lives to make the right choices, which will honour you and lead to blessing. Amen.

SEEING HIM WHO IS INVISIBLE?

These verses are the very heart of what the book is about; they bring Esther to the point of decision and they have momentous consequences. From now until the last few verses of the whole story, Esther is centre stage, and, although Mordecai continues to play a prominent part in the story, it is Esther who takes the initiative. Also, this is the part of the book that comes closest to making a theological statement and, without mentioning him, evokes God's presence and power.

The role of Esther

Even though she is queen, Esther is not indispensable: 'For if you remain silent at this time, relief and deliverance for the Jews will arise from another place' (v. 14).

It is difficult not to feel sympathy for her at this point. The options Mordecai spells out for her are stark. The temptation must have been for her to remain passive and hope for a miracle. From this point, her character blossoms and she shows complexities hitherto unexpected. Now she makes the decision that God's people are indeed her people. This was a decision that Ruth, in less dramatic circumstances, but with equally momentous consequences, also made (Ruth 1:16–17, see commentary, p. 19). God calls individuals, and, while they are never in themselves indispensable, they become part of his gracious providence. Esther, like Daniel, makes a deliberate choice to identify with God's people rather than the pagan court. Here, her decision means that she can become God's agent for rescuing his people.

Esther also acts decisively in calling a fast and in promising to go to the king (v. 16).

'Another place'

'Relief and deliverance will arise for the Jews from another place' (v. 14). The phrase 'another place' has been seen as a veiled reference to God himself, and, in later Jewish writings, is used with that meaning. In any case, it is clearly a reference to the providential outworking of events towards a conclusion. God is behind the scenes, whoever happens to be the human agent. Even in this time of disaster, God is active. This conviction runs through every part of the Bible. Indeed, it is the foundation of our faith and confidence, and without such a belief we would despair.

'For such a time as this'

The phrase 'for such a time as this' (v. 14) goes a bit further than simply speaking of the providential guiding of history. It is about God's specific guiding of human lives. There are two important things to notice in this connection. The first is that God's guidance is not mechanical or inevitable, as is shown by the question 'Who knows...?' In this world, guidance is only possible when we look with the eyes of faith, and risks are always involved. Esther was at a critical point not only in her own history but in the history of God's people and the story of salvation. Of course, it is not the case that every decision we make will have the momentous consequences of Esther's, yet, in another sense each of us is in the place that God has put us at any given time, and our actions must be seen in the light of the fulfilment of his purpose.

Taking account of providence, then, does not set aside guidance and choice. We are not robots; our choices and actions are part of the way in which God carries out his purposes. To each of us comes those moments of destiny when we know that things can never be the same again. Esther grows in stature as she shows humility instead of brash confidence that the king will listen to her. Her words 'If I perish, I perish' (v. 16) are not melodramatic; they indicate someone fully conscious of the risks but knowing that she can do nothing else. Persecution is still the experience of many Christians around the world.

The narrative is picking up speed. We are moving into a sinister world of state persecution and terrorism. Esther has already shown herself to be a woman of spirit and resourcefulness. Now, the quality called for is courage.

PRAYER

God our Father, when it comes to moments of decision, give us courage to do what is right and, depending on you, to carry out your will through Jesus Christ our Lord. Amen.

DIGNITY & DIPLOMACY

The irony of this part of the story is striking. In chapter 1, Vashti risked her life by refusing to appear before the king; now Esther risks her life by appearing unsummoned. This section begins one of the most exciting and dramatic parts of the story. There is effective use of suspense and delay in the build-up of description in verses 1–2, before we know how the king will react. Furthermore, there is a sense of menace, as the king on his royal throne emphasizes his power and absolute control, and the feeling of an approaching crisis. After verse 3, the narrative speeds up, with a sense of events moving to a climax. The 'third day' (v. 1) was the end of the fast and we wonder if this has had an effect. The sense of death and life are palpably present.

Appearances matter

We have often noticed the theme of appearance and reality in this book, but here it is rather different. This time, appearances do matter. Esther is both showing respect for the king and reminding him of the respect he owes her. Not only does she dress well, she wears her royal robes and thus shows the importance and gravity of the situation. This also is very much in line with 1 Peter 2:17: 'Show proper respect to everyone.' To dress appropriately for particular occasions, such as graduation ceremonies and weddings, is part of our Christian witness to show respect for people.

Protocol and relationships

While appearances matter, however, it is always the deeper issues of relationships and their connection with protocol that matter more. For the first time in the book, it is 'Queen Esther' who approaches the king. We are left to imagine the unspoken tension of the scene and the never-ending moment before the king raises his golden sceptre. It is a little while since the king has spoken, and when he does we find that his attitude and language have lost none of their extravagance: 'Even up to half the kingdom, it will be given you' (v. 3).

It is highly unlikely that Xerxes expected Esther to ask for what she did, any more that Herod expected his stepdaughter to ask for the head of John the Baptist when he made a similar offer. Esther's reply is shrewd and confident, and we are probably supposed to assume that fasting and praying have given her wisdom. Esther knows the unpredictability of her husband and the hold that Haman has on him. What she says is shrewd in that it appears to agree with the king's fondness for Haman and, indeed, to honour both of them. For the reader, the request for a banquet is a total surprise because, like the king, we certainly are not expecting her to ask for it. She is also tactful and does not rush into anything. Indeed, her request seems something of an anti-climax. Yet behind it is Esther's confidence that the king will respond. Indeed, she has already prepared the banquet.

A party for three

The dangerous cross-currents in the story are evident again. Verse 6 again speaks of the king drinking wine, and we are reminded of the events of chapter 1 and the rejection of Vashti. Moreover, Esther is now determined to get the king to move quickly rather than bringing in his advisers. If he is committed in advance, she has a greater chance to carry out her real plan of destroying Haman. Esther is playing a dangerous game but she has made her decision. She is in a situation of building suspense as she waits again before finally making her request. Again, the king, who has the power of life and death over her, is not actually in control. Esther's patience and wisdom are to pay off.

REFLECTION

We need patience and the ability to take the long view,
especially in confusing situations.

PRIDE BEFORE *a* FALL

The spotlight now turns on Haman, and the narrator gives us an insight into his state of mind. His moods mirror those of the king in their instability. His 'high spirits' (v. 9) reflect those of the king (1:10). But his pride and ambition blind him to the odd elements in the situation. Why should he be invited to two banquets on successive days? The repeated invitation merely swells his ego even more and makes him imagine that he is secure at the top of the pile. This part of the story has three movements.

Obsession

Haman, like the king, swings from one extreme to another. From euphoria he lurches into a crazy obsession as he sees Mordecai who, as usual, shows no sign of deference (v. 9). However, Haman is shrewd enough to hide his feelings, although they eat away at him under the surface. We may recall King Ahab's similar attitude: nothing could please him unless he could have Naboth's vineyard (1 Kings 21:1–16). Proverbs 16:18 says, 'Pride goes before destruction, a haughty spirit before a fall.' We have few better illustrations of this than Haman and his increasing hatred of Mordecai.

More advice needed

Again, like the king, Haman seeks advice, but also, like the king, since he is out of touch with reality, that advice is of little help. In his obsession he has wrongly identified Mordecai as his main opponent. He summons his wife, his friends and his family and launches into an account of how wonderful he is and how he is clearly destined for greater things yet. This section raises the whole question of advice and trust. Especially if we are in leadership, we need to be careful about those from whom we ask advice and wise in assessing the advice given. There is always a danger in simply listening to what we want to hear. Haman is a particularly extreme example, but it is a characteristic of human nature to ask advice from the people who are most likely to agree with us.

More extravagance

The gallows are ludicrously high at 23 metres (v. 14), but then every word and action of this court has been marked by extravagance. They carry echoes of the giant statue set up by Nebuchadnezzar, and are another sinister sign of pretentiousness. Ultimately the source of all such behaviour is pride, and Haman's pride is of a particularly virulent nature.

At first glance, Esther 5 seems to have little in it for the contemporary reader apart from an exciting story, although it is well-told and the characters are true to life. When we look at it in context, however, and see how the book has been developing, its importance becomes a bit clearer.

The book of Esther is a study of power and what happens when different kinds of power collide. On the surface, Haman is having his own way. He is at the height of his power, but already his inflated ego and the sense that he has lost touch with reality give warning signals. The Bible has a lot to say about power and its proper exercise. Perhaps the clearest statement occurs in 2 Samuel 23:1–7, which speaks of the importance of ruling 'in righteousness... in the fear of God' (v. 3). There is no sign of any fear in Haman, except that of losing his position. He is not fit to rule because he cannot govern his own extravagant desires. Both the king and Haman are given to impulsive and extravagant gestures, designed to impress and intimidate. On the other hand, Esther is exercising power of a very different kind, all the more effective for being understated. She is playing a dangerous game, and although she has won the first round, she may have no idea how it will end. She shows great patience, which is another form of power.

There is a sense of menace in this chapter. Again we have a reference to 'that Jew' Mordecai (v. 13), with all its implications of racial hatred. The rather vague sense of fear is spelled out in verse 14 with the specification of an extravagantly large gallows on which Mordecai will hang. Haman fondly imagines that he will have two great pleasures: the death of Mordecai and a drinking party with the king and queen.

PRAYER

God, our Father, save us from extravagance and pride,
and help us to be humble. Amen.

A BOOK *at* BEDTIME

The story moves swiftly; this is the climax of the sub-plot about Haman, which the narrator has brought centre stage. There is irony and suspense here in abundance and a clever interweaving of character and plot. A number of interesting clues indicate the significance of this little episode.

Another 'coincidence'?

In a way characteristic of this whole story, we now have another coincidence, an apparently minor event which is to have profound consequences. The king's sleeplessness is to be the trigger of the events in this chapter. Esther is not the only place in scripture where such events take place: in the Joseph story (Genesis 41—43), similar 'coincidences' occur; and in Daniel 6, King Darius cannot sleep while Daniel is in the lions' den. There are many differences between these stories, however, not least that in both Genesis and Daniel the theological issues of God's providential control of events, however trivial they may seem, are made explicit.

Here, in verse 1, the king asks for the history of his reign to be read to him. The intention was to send him to sleep, but in fact it spurs him to action. He could no doubt have found many other diversions but providence is at work. Xerxes' actions are not ultimately his own idea: there is another player behind the scenes. The narrative is crisply told and the clash between Mordecai and Haman is given a new twist.

'Sleep fled'

'Sleep fled' is what the text literally says (v. 1), and we wonder why. Did the king perhaps have strange dreams and an uneasy conscience? This is hardly the stuff of which history is made, but it is nevertheless part of the pattern of events. Strictly speaking, there is no such thing as a 'coincidence': as we look at the world around us, and at our own lives, we need to see them with the eye of faith and realize that everything is significant, even though it may not seem so at the time. It seems incredible that a sleepless night should be the rock on which Haman's plot was wrecked, but that is how it was. This does not mean that we shall always, or even often, see the meaning of every event; it does mean, however, that we have a God who is in control.

Links to the main plot

Xerxes asks (v. 3) what 'honour and recognition' Mordecai has received. The same words (translated as 'splendour and glory') are used in 1:4 about the kingdom of Persia, when Xerxes is showing off his wealth and splendour to his guests. The 'record of his reign' that is read to the king is a further reminder of the background against which this whole story is unfolding. It is a story about the affairs of nations as well as individuals. The whole pattern of events matters to God.

In many ways, this little episode is a window into the meaning of the book, and it is worth pausing for a moment to look at it more closely.

We are back again in the world of chapter 1, where power was seen in terms of conquered countries, vast wealth, extravagant furnishings and prodigious eating and drinking. All the questions raised about where power really lies are now brought to the fore again. We saw how hollow was the appearance of power, and we suspect that the same may be true here as well.

We are also in a world where no certainty is possible. The shifting alliances, intrigues and counter-intrigues at the heart of all centres of power make for uncertainty and fear. In this situation, living by faith is the only way to find a power greater than that of the world.

The book of Esther is shot through with the sense of God working behind the scenes. He never appears directly, but only the conviction of his unseen presence makes any sense of the diverse events and apparent coincidences.

REFLECTION

Ponder the many coincidences in your life and thank God that he is always working behind the scenes.

RISING & FALLING

The story moves swiftly as Haman, puffed up with pride, comes into the royal presence, no doubt expecting further honours, and at first it seems that this is exactly what is going to happen (v. 6). The king summons him immediately and invites him to suggest some special reward for the royal favourite. Haman launches into the most exaggerated scene he can imagine, supposing that he is the one to be favoured; in fact, he wants to masquerade publicly as king. The sudden dashing of his hopes as he is ordered to honour Mordecai is a supreme example of irony (v. 10).

The danger of pride

Haman's pride—like so much else in this book—is gigantic, and it is to be followed by a total reversal of circumstances. Yet we must not assume that it has nothing to say to us. It is of the essence of pride to be extravagant and to blind us to reality. Pride is, essentially, making ourselves gods. In most people's lives, this will show itself in all kinds of ways: desire for recognition, over-dependence on money or possessions, resentment of the success of others. God gives us good gifts and it is important to be thankful for them, but when we forget that they are gifts and treat them as personal possessions, we fall into pride. Because Haman was in a position of great power, his pride had huge consequences, but all of our pride has consequences in all kinds of ways. Pride leads to presumption and to a feeling of invulnerability; we need to learn from Haman the danger of such an attitude.

Mordecai vindicated

Paradoxically, the honours Haman lusted after are now showered on his worst enemy—the last man to be impressed by such a display. We are told nothing of Mordecai's reaction to this unexpected turn of events. His people are still under a death sentence, and when it is all over he simply returns to the king's gate (v. 12). There is no sense of triumphalism on his part. He knows very well how fickle the moods of the king are, and makes no attempt to exploit his temporary elevation. The phrase 'Mordecai the Jew' (v. 10) reminds us of the main plot of the story, which is still unfolding and to which we shall return.

Dismal advice

We have reached a critical point in this sub-plot. Haman may still be able to extricate himself; we do not yet know what Esther, who is absent from this chapter, will do. On the surface, all remains as it was back in chapter 3, when Xerxes promoted Haman. The edict against the Jews stands, and maybe the establishment will be strong enough to crush any opposition.

We have noticed how much of the action in the story includes taking advice, especially on the part of the king. We have also noted that this advice is seldom useful and seldom followed. The advice that Haman is now given by his wife and friends is dismal in the extreme, though, ironically, it is sound. They dissociate themselves from him: 'you cannot stand against [Mordecai]' (v. 13). Although the edict against them still stands, the Jewish people no longer seem such an endangered minority. The honouring of Mordecai is a kind of acted parable of how the main plot is going to develop, and the drama increases as the king's eunuchs arrive and Haman is 'hurried away' to the next banquet before he can finish his conversation. Events are overtaking him and control is slipping from his hands.

The structure of the chapter reinforces the underlying message. It begins and ends with two powerful men, disturbed and unable to steer events. In between, both of them—one willingly, the other not —honour a man who, in spite of appearances, is about to be handed control.

We have already noticed, in 3:12, the echoes of the exodus narrative (see commentary, p. 58). That might have led us to imagine that God, who had worked spectacularly then, would do so again here to rescue his people. Rescue is to come, but it will arrive through the 'normal' events and circumstances as they unfold.

PRAYER

God our Father, in the puzzling circumstances of life help us to trust in your purposes of love and to walk the way of faith. Amen.

ESTHER IN CONTROL

Here we reach the climax of the sub-plot and the demise of Haman. This section is marked by a further demonstration of Esther's coolness and calm control of the situation. The storytelling art we have come to expect from this author is evident again. Esther is described as 'Queen Esther' and addressed so by Xerxes (v. 2) as in 5:3. Indeed, he repeats exactly the words he used at the previous banquet. Esther replies with elaborate courtesy, and now introduces the fact that it is her people and not herself that concern her (v. 3). She skilfully continues (v. 4), using the passive voice and not revealing the villain's true identity. Then, when she reveals who the villain is, it has all the intensity and excitement of a dramatic and spectacular reversal.

A number of main issues emerge from this episode. The first is revealed in verse 4: 'I and my people have been sold.' 'Sold' refers in the first place to the money Haman offered to the king (3:9), but it also has echoes of being sold into slavery and is a reminder to the reader that the Israelites were once slaves in Egypt and that they are in a similar danger again. This is a crisis in the history of God's people. The actions of Esther are used by God to ensure that his people are saved; she has indeed come to the kingdom for such a time as this.

The second issue is the nature of Esther's role. We have already looked at the naivety of seeing Esther as a role model (see commentary on 2:12–18, pp. 52–53). The narrator, then as now, makes no comment on the incident and tells nothing about Esther's state of mind. There is little point in speculating on this. The issue of how to respond to an aggressor faces leaders at all times, especially in situations of war, and we shall discuss it further in chapter 9.

Third, the spotlight again falls on the king, who reacts in the way we have come to expect of him. When Haman is exposed, the king finds himself at a loss; no advisors are present. He is extravagant in his anger as he is in everything else. It is significant too that he is far more concerned that he should have been betrayed in his own house (v. 8) and have had his dignity affronted than that thousands of people are going to perish. He does not think or consider; he simply reacts.

Fourth, the major concern of the chapter is the downfall of Haman. Once again, there is no gloating over this outcome, but there is irony.

Haman's fate is richly deserved, yet it is for one of the few crimes he did not commit that he was condemned (v. 8). Indeed, sexual sins do not seem to have figured at all in Haman's all-consuming lust for power. Swift and merciless judgment falls on him and he is destroyed by the system he so ruthlessly manipulated to destroy others. Just as in Daniel 6 the conspirators were destroyed in the den they designed to overwhelm Daniel, so here Haman falls into his own trap.

There is a principle here that runs through scripture, namely, that judgment is not arbitrary and is closely related to character and action. Proverbs 11:8, for example, is illustrated by this story of Mordecai and Haman—'The righteous man is rescued from trouble, and it comes on the wicked instead'—as is Matthew 7:2: 'For in the same way that you judge others, you will be judged.' The king acted in a headstrong, unscrupulous and extravagant way, but that was the kind of king Haman wanted him to be, the better to manipulate him. The judgment of God comes when God allows us to have what we want and it ultimately destroys us.

Moreover, evil has a self-destructive aspect. Up until now in Esther, and so often in our world today, evil appears to be in entire control and monolithic in its threat to God's people. Look at the exposure of evil in Revelation 17, however, and see how the powers of darkness turn against each other: 'The beast and the ten horns you saw will hate the prostitute' (17:16). When God is at work, the opposition begins to fragment and part of its judgment is mutual hatred.

Once again, something that, on the surface, is simply a well-told story of intrigue and the machinations of power politics turns out to be a window into God's purposes. It is a reminder not to be intimidated by evil, nor to trust those in power too much. At root, evil is pride, a sense of being in charge of people and circumstances with no need to 'act justly and to love mercy and to walk humbly with your God' (Micah 6:8). This leads to a life centred on one's own position, comfort and ambition, and a contempt for others. One day God will usher in a new heaven and a new earth, where evil will be banished; until then, we need to recognize and resist it.

PRAYER

Lord, give us the vision to see you at work in the world, and the faith to believe that your kingdom will come. Amen.

POLITICAL REVERSALS

The sub-plot is over but there is much unfinished business. The issue of the edict to destroy the Jews (3:12) remains unresolved. The removal of Haman has not solved the problem. A victory has been won but the main battle has still to be fought. This is a characteristic of the life of faith.

The significance of Mordecai

Until now, Mordecai has had great status, but now he is given effective power. The signet ring (v. 2) gives the bearer power to act on the king's behalf; indeed, it was last given to Haman (3:10) when he set in motion the chain of events that Mordecai is now seeking to reverse. There is great formality here in verses 1–2, showing that we are moving from the intensely personal to the overtly political. The major theme of chapter 8 is reversals, which continue into chapter 9.

The role of Esther

Here, Esther is involved both politically and personally. She hands over her newly acquired estate to Mordecai, and this decisively completes the reversal of his and Haman's fortunes (v. 2). More personally and passionately, she pleads with Xerxes to undo the effects of Haman's evil plan (v. 3). Once again she combines shrewdness with emotion and omits all reference to the king's own part in issuing the edict. She emphasizes her relationship to her people and the way her destiny is bound up with theirs. She carefully avoids exaggerating the danger and comes to the point quickly.

The reaction of Xerxes

Once again, Xerxes is the victim of the elaborate state mechanism of which he is theoretically master and, as is his habit, he tries to evade responsibility. As he has done since chapter 1, he also tries to find a way out of the problem that makes it look as if he wields absolute power. He puts the onus on Esther to find a way out of the dilemma, thinking correctly that she will probably succeed.

Once again, a number of important principles lie behind the narrative. The overriding theme is the providence of God, using people and circumstances. He does not act contrary to people's personalities; rather, he uses their attitudes and behaviour to bring about his purposes, here to reverse the edict of Haman.

The question of power, which is another of the leading themes of the book, is treated here in a fascinating way. The king, who is the *de jure* source of all power in the kingdom, shows total inability and indeed lack of concern to find a solution to the problem he has created by his advancement of Haman. Esther has again shown the power both of principle and of personality. Power is profoundly ambiguous. Haman has used it for evil purposes and, in so doing, has destroyed himself. The king, while he has power, has no idea how to use it. The final chapters of the book will explore the ambiguities of power further.

Another important theme is solidarity: 'For how can I bear to see disaster fall on my people? How can I bear to see the destruction of my family?' (v. 6). Esther has irrevocably committed herself to her people and their destiny. Both she and Mordecai are now in such a position that, whatever an edict said, no one could dare to attack them personally. However, they show great loyalty and solidarity with their people and will not rest easily until measures have been taken to save them. God's purposes for his people are irrevocable (as Paul says in Romans 11:29), but he does use humans to carry out his purposes.

REFLECTION

God places us in circumstances and gives us opportunities. How we use them will shape our lives and the lives of others.

REVERSALS *of* EDICT & MOOD

The story moves swiftly in this section, and verse 9 reminds us of 3:12–15, when the then Prime Minister Haman issued the original decree. The date of the new edict is 70 days later than Haman's edict; we may have here a veiled allusion to the 70 years of exile.

The extent of the killing

Verse 11 has caused a great deal of heart-searching among commentators. First, there is a translation issue. Haman's decree in 3:13 ordered the merciless destruction of all the Jews, including women and children. This decree of Mordecai appears to sanction the killing of women and children among the enemies of the Jews (as in AV and RSV). The NIV and a minority of commentators read the text to mean that the 'women and children' mentioned are themselves Jewish, and thus the instruction is to kill any armed force that might attack the Jews *and their women and children*. The issue cannot be discussed fully here and interested readers are referred to the commentaries mentioned in the Further Reading section (pp. 14–15). However, given the author's habit of presenting events in parallel and as reversals, it seems likely that the traditional reading is correct and that Mordecai's decree does license the killing of women and children.

What are we to make of the moral issue involved in the slaughter of these innocent people? The first thing to remember is where Esther comes in the overall canon of scripture. Ancient Israel was a political entity and had to operate in the world of its day. The cross and resurrection of Jesus dealt the death blow to the powers of evil, and we live under a new covenant where forgiveness is at the heart of relationships.

In the context of the Old Testament, we have to remember how we have been reading this narrative. Mordecai and Esther are not primarily presented as models for us to follow. They play their part in the story of salvation, and God overrules, whether what they do is admirable or not. Tied up with this is the fundamental issue of God's judgment and how this works for his purposes through the choices and decisions that people make. We shall explore this further in chapter 9.

The atmosphere of party

Verses 15–18 are a reversal of mood in this story of reversals. Mordecai's colourful royal robes recall Esther's similar appearance in 5:1. This is a reversal of 4:3, with feasting replacing mourning and fasting, not only in the capital of Susa but throughout the provinces. What is even more remarkable is the conversion of many people to Judaism (v. 17). This recalls earlier parts of the Bible, such as Joshua 2:9. We do not know how genuine these conversions were. Many people, at least, would probably convert from expediency (we all like to join the winning side), although 9:27 suggests that some converts were genuine. It is an important reminder that, even in Old Testament times, Jewish identity was never simply a matter of race. The prophets looked to a day when many from all over the world would turn to God (see, for example, Isaiah 2:2–4; Jeremiah 3:17; Zephaniah 3:9; Zechariah 8:22–23).

This chapter could well have ended the book, but in a sense the most significant part is still to come, and the festival that commemorates the events has still to be described. There are still also unresolved tensions and questions of vengeance and 'holy war' to be explored further in chapter 9.

PRAYER

God our Father, help us to bloom where you have planted us and to be faithful in our everyday lives. Amen.

The STORY IS NOT OVER

Without this chapter and the short chapter 10, the story of Esther would simply fizzle out. Both in terms of completing the story and of bringing out the theological significance, these chapters are vital for an overall understanding of the book.

The day arrives

At last the 13th of Adar, the day appointed for the massacre of the Jews, has arrived. The wording of 3:12–13 is again echoed, under-lining the overwhelming nature of the reversal of fortune that has happened. Mordecai now has the power of life and death over his enemies. He is the embodiment of the change that has happened. The 'fear' that fell on people (v. 3) is unexplained but there is plainly a supernatural element involved, and in the total biblical context we can say that it is the 'fear of God', which is the beginning of wisdom (Psalm 111:10). The reversal of fortune that had happened for Mordecai now happens for the Jews as a whole. Again no particular explanations are given; we are left to infer that the providence of God is at work.

Killing and more killing

Undoubtedly, what makes the reader most uneasy is the extent of the killing. First of all, we must not exaggerate what happened. This was battle, not simply wanton massacre, and was probably less than what would have happened to the Jews if Haman's decree had been carried out and they had been unable to defend themselves. Although 75,000 (v. 16) is a huge number, it must be seen in the light of the fact that it was spread over 127 provinces of the empire with a huge population.

The king's response to the killing once again shows his insensi-tivity. In verse 12 he promises Esther to give her what she wants, this time in relation to the killing. He is unshaken by the slaughter and indifferent to more of it happening. He has no concern for his own people any more than he had for the Jews.

What is more difficult is Esther's request for a second day of killing and the hanging of the dead bodies of Haman's sons. It is important to notice that the author neither commends nor condemns Esther here. This is not an example to follow but an account of what happened. In a fallen world there is always the danger of excess and of seeking revenge rather than security.

There are further points to consider. The first is that the phrase 'they did what they pleased to those who hated them' (v. 5) probably does not mean that the Jews acted with excessive cruelty but that they acted without any official interference. Second, it is emphasized that the Jews took no plunder (vv. 10, 15, 16). It is just possible that this may represent a glance at earlier history. Abraham refused to accept the plunder offered him by the king of Sodom (Genesis 14:21–23). On the other hand, Saul selected the best animals for himself after the defeat of Agag and the Amalekites (1 Samuel 15:13–15).

This episode clearly raises many questions, not least about the exercise of power. It is difficult for human beings to exercise power consistently and fairly. The temptation is always to be either overbearing or indulgent. We have continually to remember the place of Esther in the whole unfolding canon. Only in Christ himself will we have a perfect blend of fearless execution of divine justice and the gentleness which is the mask of true strength.

The other issue is the one that has run like an underground river throughout the story: the providence of God. Often it works through changing hearts and minds, although that does not happen here. Rather, God works through the messy business of politics and war. Once again, this has to be fitted into the whole story of salvation where, through the cross and resurrection, evil is given its death blow and a new heaven and new earth are made certain.

PRAYER

Lord God, if you give us any position of power or influence, help us to be humble and to use what you have given us to honour your name and help others. Amen.

A New Festival

The story is almost over, but the theme of joy and feasting, so common in the book, has been introduced again. What has happened is now to be remembered and institutionalized in a new festival. This story 'from Persian lands afar' is to take its place along with the festivals instituted by Moses in the Pentateuch as a celebration of another of God's acts of faithfulness.

Its origin

'Therefore these days were called Purim, from the word *pur*' (v. 26). Haman had cast the *pur*, a kind of die or lot, as he planned the downfall of the Jews. This is yet another reminder that the lot of God's people would not be decided by Haman casting lots before his own gods. Underlying it were the written words of Mordecai (v. 20), which established this festival as an annual part of Jewish life and legislated for its continuance (vv. 27–28). The first festival was a spontaneous overflow of relief and thankfulness, and thus it was never forgotten.

Its nature

At the heart of Purim is celebration—not the godless celebration of chapter 1, which is marked by unbounded excess and leads directly to the unpleasant events of the book, but true joy based on gratitude. Today it lasts long into the night and the emphasis is on feasting and laughter. Some commentators refer to the popularity of Esther during the Holocaust, and the hatred the Nazis felt for the book.

Its significance

Some commentators have criticized what they see as repetition in this section, particularly in verses 23–25, with its reiteration of some details of the story, and in verses 29–32, which seem to be an unnecessary repeat of verses 20–22. What is being done is, in fact, something rather different. Human beings have a tendency to forget when danger is past, so people need to be continually reminded. Written records are important in keeping past events and their present significance before our minds. This festival is also a powerful reminder in times of prosperity to trust in God and not in favourable circumstances. The significance of the festival and the events that engendered it is emphasized by Queen Esther and Mordecai writing a letter to give it 'full authority' (v. 29). Not only does the letter become part of the law of Persia, it also becomes part of the written scripture, and is described as 'words of goodwill and assurance' (v. 30). These words point beyond the immediate circumstances of the book and point to the heart of the gospel, with its message of goodwill to all.

Esther is part of the canon of scripture that God has given to his people in all ages, to help them to live the life of faith. In the Psalter, people are continually called to remember God's mighty acts and to 'forget not all his benefits' (Psalm 103:2). In the Lord's Supper we remember Calvary and proclaim the Lord's death until he comes. This book, like the rest of the Bible, has future perspective: the defeat of Haman is an anticipation of the day when all God's enemies will be destroyed. As we have seen, it also looks back to the exodus and thus forms an important link in the whole story of salvation.

PRAYER

As we remember God's goodness, these words from
Psalm 104:33–34 are appropriate:

'I will sing to the Lord as long as I live; I will sing praise to my
God while I have being. May my meditation be pleasing to him,
for I rejoice in the Lord.'

Bowing Out

We return to normal life, if that is the appropriate phrase to use.

The king back in control

Xerxes returns to the concerns of empire after what he had probably only seen as 'a little local difficulty'. The word translated 'tribute' or 'tax' in verse 1 sometimes implies conscription to forced labour, so behind this laconic statement lies a whole world of oppression and poverty. He is fully back in control—or is he? Xerxes' power has been systematically deconstructed and there is no reason to believe that the apparently universal control he exercises here is any more substantial than his earlier authority. The kingdom of God has briefly made its presence felt and nothing can ever be the same again.

Another book

In verse 2 we find mentioned the official history of Media and Persia, perhaps a chronological account covering a number of centuries. Mordecai now enjoys a status comparable to that of Joseph at the court of Pharaoh. This is a reminder that we are dealing with history and not legend. Mordecai's status was no temporary phenomenon. Once again the act of writing endows the situation with solidity and permanence.

Mordecai and his people

As the curtain falls, we find that Mordecai is exercising power with humility and generosity, and the Jews are now living in harmony and peace with their Gentile neighbours.

In the book of Esther we have probably the supreme biblical example of the life of faith at its most minimalistic and on the farthest edges. As we have seen, there are no prophets, no ritual worship, no specific references to God himself, no overt praying and certainly no miracles. Yet, just beneath the surface, the life of faith is being lived. That is why this story is so valuable for our lives. For most of us, life goes on without apparent intervention from God. Most of the time the sea does not open up before us, miracles do not rain down from the skies and we do not see unmistakable evidence of God at work.

It is a powerful reminder that the life of faith can be lived in the most unpromising of circumstances.

We also see here a fine dramatization of God's sovereignty and human responsibility. The characters in the story make choices freely, yet God uses those choices to work out his purposes. We have also seen this in the book of Ruth (see especially commentary on Ruth 2 and 3, pp. 22–33).

It is a reminder too that God still cared for those who remained in Babylon and Persia when Cyrus allowed the Jews to return to their homeland.

In conclusion, this book has many important things to say about power, relationships and behaviour. As has been emphasized, though, what we have here is not a model to be followed exactly but shrewd and dramatic pictures of how people behave and what influences shape their lives. In particular, we learn how God's people can operate in a hostile environment and even rise to positions of great influence. Similar issues are raised in the stories of Joseph and Daniel, although there the hand of God is specifically seen at work. The issues of when to compromise, when to take a stand and how to judge human nature are prominent in the book of Esther, which is a great human document.

REFLECTION

Reflect on these words by A.T Pierson:

'Man proposes. God disposes; all things his design fulfil;
Every human wrath unconscious serves to execute his will.
So man's festival of Purim, read in faith's illumined sense,
Shall be seen in realms eternal as the feast of Providence.'

MR PREACHER FAILS *to* CHARM

Wilfred Owen, killed by a sniper's bullet a week before the Armistice in 1918, wrote a number of poignant and beautiful poems about the Great War. One of these, 'Futility', speaks of his sorrow at finding the dead body of a young soldier, 'limbs still warm'. Owen reflects on the soldier's all-too-brief past and non-existent future, and this leads on to a wilder sense of futility at the origin and purpose of creation:

> *O what made fatuous sunbeams toil,*
> *To break earth's sleep at all?*

That is the world of Ecclesiastes. It is more than private grief; it is a profound weariness and pessimism at the futility, the vanity, the meaninglessness of the universe. What is this book doing in the Bible and what are we going to make of it?

Who was he?

The title 'Ecclesiastes' in our English Bible, which comes to us from the Latin translation, is very inappropriate. A less ecclesiastical or churchy person than our author is hard to imagine. In verse 1 he is called 'Teacher' or 'Preacher', and there is an increasing tendency for writers on this book simply to use the Hebrew term *Qoheleth*, which is a word with no exact English equivalent. The word means someone who calls an assembly together to address it. A whole variety of titles have been suggested—Preacher, Teacher, Lecturer, Spokesman, Professor and the like—while some have opted for the Americanism 'Mr Preacher'. In any case, here we have teaching about the meaning of life, and before launching into this, Mr Preacher gives us his credentials.

He is 'son of David, king in Jerusalem'. This places him at the very heart of Israel's life, yet what he has to say comes from the edge, and places profound question marks against mainstream faith. The use of the mysterious name *Qoheleth* distances him from the centre, and is the first of the book's many riddles. This suggests that 'Mr Preacher' is not Solomon himself but someone assuming his mantle. 'Suppose,' says our author, 'I had the power, intelligence, wealth, opportunities, shrewdness and experiences of Solomon, what would life be like? Could I, with all advantages, make a go of it?'

Dating the book is difficult and depends on many uncertainties, such as the kind of Hebrew language used. Some see it as a product of the exile and the gloom and misery of that time. Knowledge about date is not essential to its appreciation, however.

What is he saying?

Qoheleth's answer is singularly bleak. Everything is *hebel*, meaning 'breath, vapour, mist, vanity, futility, what is empty'. Four times in quick succession we are told that everything is 'meaningless'. The author is out to strip us of all illusions and force us to face up to reality. The rest of the book will analyse meaninglessness wherever it is found, amid all the most rewarding, fulfilling and exciting experiences that life has to offer. What is our author about?

First, he is determined to give human wisdom, power and pleasure a run for their money. Not for him easy platitudes and clever soundbites. He will not cater to our longing for easy answers and comfortable illusions. As we shall see, he writes with a poetic wistfulness and beauty that testify to the human longing for fulfilment.

Second, his book is a kind of pre-evangelism. One of the commentators calls it a 'John the Baptist' kind of book. By demonstrating the final emptiness of life without God, it forces us to consider him.

Third, Ecclesiastes is going to ask profound questions about creation, and we will find many links with Genesis 1—11. If everything is meaningless, we have to consider whether we are in a universe that just happens to be there, without cause or explanation. If that is so, then the book will be one of unrelieved pessimism. If, however, this condition is a consequence of the judgment of God and thus within God's power to relieve, then we shall read it with excitement and explanation.

The association of Ecclesiastes with the feast of Tabernacles or Booths links a sombre book with a joyful festival. The feast of Tabernacles both celebrates the fruitfulness of harvest and remembers the desert wanderings of Israel. Both parts of the celebration would remind people of their vulnerability and dependence on God. Without such goodness and dependability, life is indeed meaningless.

PRAYER

Lord, take away our illusions and false hopes and help us to build on your rock, to depend on you, the bountiful giver, and to find meaning and purpose in you and in your great love for us.

NOTHING MAKES SENSE

As Mr Preacher develops his thesis, he ransacks both the material world and human experience to find examples that demonstrate the truth of his pessimism. He develops this in three areas.

Personal life

Life is characterized as 'labour' and 'toil' (v. 3), words that suggest both the physical effort and the mental anguish often associated with work. Here for the first time occurs the characteristic phrase 'under the sun'. The perspective is crystallized in the word 'gain', which is a commercial term and implies that the meaning of life is to be found in profit and in demonstrable results. The question 'What does man gain…?' receives no direct answer; the next few verses imply that personal life simply reflects the greater lack of purpose writ large throughout time and space.

This sense of pointlessness is underlined by verse 4, which contrasts the brevity and repeated disappearance of human generations with the apparent stability and permanence of the earth. 'Forever', used of the earth, implies that earthly futility has no obvious end or hope of improvement. It is instructive to compare this idea with Psalm 102:24–28, where the physical universe is said to wear out and to be laid aside like discarded clothes, while God's servants will remain for ever. The psalmist's perspective is of the eternal kingship of God, however, while in Ecclesiastes no such conviction seems real 'under the sun'.

Creation

Like human life, the created order is full of activity, yet none of it reveals a purpose or leads to a consummation (vv. 5–7). The psalmists are full of praise for God's beauty and glory in nature (see, for example, Psalms 19; 90; 104), but here we have the exact opposite. In Psalm 19:5 the sun is like a warrior running a race with vigour, but here (v. 5) the verb translated 'hurries' would be better rendered as 'gasps' or 'pants', and is used of an exhausted runner. Similarly the wind, described with the use of participles—'going/turning' and 'turning/going' (v. 6)—gives a sense of wearisome monotony. The rivers, which in Psalm 98:8 'clap their hands', are here (v. 7) simply another example of repetitive and purposeless activity. All of this results in verse 8 in a jaded, exhausted and unfulfilled frustration.

History

'Under the sun', time is no better than space. The flow of history has about it the same wearisome repetitiveness as nature (vv. 9–11). History is a closed circuit that neither effort nor new events can change. The idea that there is such a thing as novelty is only evidence of a lack of knowledge of the past: that past is soon forgotten and the present will likewise follow it into oblivion. 'Remembrance', in the biblical sense, is not simply calling something to mind; rather, it means remembering and acting accordingly. Thus there is nothing on which to look back with satisfaction or forwards with hope.

The author has certainly forced us to face up to the consequences of a worldview confined to what is 'under the sun'. Creation has no power to excite or inspire and history has no lessons to be learnt. We cannot look backward, forward or upward; indeed, the only place we can look is inside, and there we simply see reflected the futility of all time and space.

This book is very useful in pre-evangelism. It shows soberly and clearly what the world is like when we leave God out of the picture. Like John the Baptist, it reveals our need and thus impels us to Christ, who alone can meet that need. Our author will go beyond what he says here, but he is concerned to make us face the sheer pointlessness of life without God. Here there is no sense of history going somewhere, and the whole universe seems to have no meaning.

Much of this resonates with our own experience. In the political scene, leaders who were once household names are soon forgotten and others take their place who, in future generations, will suffer a similar oblivion. Similarly, those who work in institutions such as colleges know how quickly the fleeting generations forget those who were once at the centre of the institution's life.

Mr Preacher will have more to say than this, but facing up to the reality he so powerfully depicts is a necessary foundation for hearing what comes later.

REFLECTION

We need to be honest about the futility of life 'under the sun' before we can appreciate what Christ offers.

The DESPERATE SEARCH

Our author now turns from observation to experience. Assuming the mantle of Solomon, he now puts to the test the thesis of verses 1 and 2. If someone has the power, brains, wealth and opportunities of Solomon, would it be possible to make a success of life 'under the sun'? The author is not boasting; it is a sober statement of his talents and opportunities and a serious attempt to find the meaning of life.

For the first time in the book, God is mentioned (v. 13). In one sense, what the author says is wholly orthodox: he sees God as responsible for human life, here described as 'a heavy burden'. The role of God is to be of increasing significance throughout the book. The Preacher sets himself a daunting task: he is exploring 'all that is done under heaven', which involves a total worldview. As yet, this worldview is horizontal, although the mention of God hints at the vertical dimension which is to come. 'I devoted myself' (v. 13) is more exactly rendered 'I set my heart', suggesting that his whole personality and inner self is involved in the search. The word 'study' means to search deeply, and the word 'explore' means to search widely. Thus this investigation is to have both depth and breadth.

He begins with the idea that life is a heavy burden, and then quotes a proverb that emphasizes the impossibility of finding a regular pattern in the universe (v. 15). There is no way to straighten out the anomalies or make good what is deficient. He applies this proverb in two particular spheres, as follows.

The failure of wisdom

A lesser man might have settled for less, but Mr Preacher sees that wisdom has in fact magnified the problem. His wisdom and experience are not in doubt and he is well aware that they are different from folly. Yet the crushing realization is that the end result of wisdom is the same as that of folly: 'a chasing after the wind'. This echoes 1:6 about the futile and repetitive ways in which the wind goes about the world. Indeed, wisdom magnifies the problem (v. 18) because it strips away illusions and makes the futility of life more obvious. Wisdom brings 'sorrow' (more exactly, 'frustration'), and knowledge brings 'grief' as the sorry business of life becomes clearer.

The failure of hedonism

If wisdom has failed, then pleasure beckons. The conclusion is first given (2:1) and then it is substantiated. Hedonism is introduced by two different words, 'laughter' and 'pleasure'. 'Laughter' is used of games, parties and other amusements. 'Pleasure' is often used of the joy of religious festivals or of gratitude. But all such feelings and occasions, whether superficial or highbrow, fail to satisfy. Our author now gives examples of activities that are associated with pleasure.

Drinking wine is not wrong in itself (indeed, it is commended in 9:7) and our author specifically says that he drank it, 'my mind still guiding me with wisdom' (v. 3). He is trying to loosen his inhibitions and see if wine will help him in his search for the good life. This is a persistent quest: 'I wanted to see what was worthwhile'.

He now turns to his projects (v. 4): more literally, 'I made great my works'. These are building projects: houses, vineyards and gardens with all their associations of pleasant living, luxury and beautiful surroundings. In particular, he dwells on the gardens, while the pools and forest echo Eden (Genesis 2:9–10). Qoheleth is describing an attempt to build an earthly paradise; he wants to be master over nature. He also wants to be a lord over people—'I bought males and female slaves'—and over animals—'I also owned more herds and flocks than anyone in Jerusalem before me' (v. 7). East of Eden, he is attempting to exercise the dominion given to unfallen humans. He also acquires great material wealth and sexual satisfaction on a vast scale (v. 8). All this he claims to have done without losing wisdom, although we should remember that wisdom can be ungodly as well. He has denied himself nothing, has thoroughly enjoyed himself and has gained reward (v. 10).

But what was the end result? Hedonism failed to bring satisfaction. Mr Preacher's key terms are used again: 'toil', 'chasing after wind', 'meaningless' (v. 11). The combination of these words shows his disillusionment and bitter frustration.

PRAYER

Teach us to number our days aright,
that we may gain a heart of wisdom.

Psalm 90:12

IS IT WORTH IT?

Our author is now summing up his opening reflections on wisdom and folly. He has thought deeply both on the created order and on human activity and has pursued vigorously all that life has to offer. Now he stands back and gives us his observations. He is far from a solution, but some interesting points emerge.

Hints of a way ahead

The section begins with a sober realization that if Solomon could not make it, 'what more can the king's successor do?' (v. 12). Excessive indulgence and amazing opportunities, in the end, amount to little and are, like everything else, merely repetitive. When he compares wisdom and folly to light and darkness, however, he sets us moving into a different dimension. This is reminiscent of passages in Proverbs such as 4:18–19: 'The path of the righteous is like the first gleam of dawn, shining ever brighter till the full light of day. But the way of the wicked is like deep darkness; they do not know what makes them stumble.' Plainly wisdom has some value and is not to be despised, but this is not the final answer.

The fact of death

The reason that wisdom is not the final answer is that it is of little use if there is no one to exercise it. Death makes no distinction between the wise and the foolish; nor is the wise person more likely to be remembered than the fool (v. 16). Death is the great leveller, and from the perspective of 'under the sun' there is no escape. Yet *Qoheleth* is raising questions of ultimate significance and this in turn raises the possibility that there are issues which cannot be resolved 'under the sun'.

What is work about?

The overwhelming reality of death causes our author to hate life (v. 17). He focuses here on the sheer effort of work and its unproductiveness. This is in the same vein as Genesis 3:17–19, where part of the judgment on Adam is that work will be tedious and painful. What particularly annoys Mr Preacher is that someone who comes after him will reap the benefits that have eluded him. Work has become a dead end and, while absorbing all his time, brings no satisfaction. So much of this rings bells in our own day. People are working harder than ever, until work takes over, and yet it brings no lasting satisfaction.

Plainly *Qoheleth* is not simply thinking of work, however; it is the whole of life that seems immeasurably dreary and pointless. This is particularly plain in verse 23: 'All his days his work is pain and grief; even at night his mind does not rest. This too is meaningless.' All of his days and nights have been gripped with a sense of futility and utter frustration.

A glimmer of hope

Verses 24–26 are rather more optimistic. We should notice first that God is mentioned three times, underlining the conviction that he is behind all the mystery of the world. This is both liberating and alarming. Here wisdom is not acquired; it is God's gift. Words such as 'satisfaction', enjoyment' and 'happiness' point to a realm beyond the grey world in which we have been trapped. This reflects the creation narratives of Genesis 1 and 2, where the earth is essentially 'good' (and this is not only true of the unfallen world, for it is echoed in Psalm 104:31). Moreover, God judges; this is the implication of 'gives' in verse 26, and to those who do not please him this is loss. Ultimately this is a eschatological perspective, and it is probable that the 'meaningless' of verse 26 applies to the 'sinner' rather than to one who 'pleases God'.

These verses are significant. They echo what Deuteronomy 30:15–20 says about obeying or disobeying the covenant. 'See, I set before you today life and prosperity, death and destruction.'

Once introduced into the flow of the book, God cannot simply be ignored. We are not yet at the conclusion, but we now have another perspective, another possible way of living. If we omit God, every road will end in a cul-de-sac, but there is another way—the way of pleasing God. That way, life is a gift rather than a burden. We are no longer trapped in the space/time universe.

REFLECTION

Life throws up choices, and we need to try to hear the voice of God and follow his way.

A TIME *for* EVERYTHING

Few things fascinate us as much as time. Time travel is a constant theme in science-fiction and reflects our sense of the irreversibly lost past and the unknown future. We continually express surprise at the swift passage of time, as if we were not really at home in it (see 1:11). We never have enough of it, yet it can hang heavily on our hands. It is hardly surprising that our author, as he continues to reflect on life, now turns to time.

Verses 1–8 are a beautiful and moving poem, charting human experience from cradle to grave. There are two ways in which this section can be understood, however. First, we might say that time is simply another example of 'meaninglessness', an arbitrary tyrant that continually disrupts plans and makes planned and ordered life impossible. In a real sense, we are 'serving time' and our life sentence is relentless and pointless. If we have been right in discerning a note of optimism at the end of chapter 2, though, that interpretation sounds unconvincing.

Thus, the second possible interpretation of the section seems more probable, that it is a celebration of the unceasing and glorious variety that God provides in life. In 14 couplets, the author covers the whole of human activity, using the characteristic Old Testament method of expressing comparisons by means of polar opposites. Verse 1 makes a general statement, which is illustrated in different spheres in verses 2–8.

Beginnings and endings

In verse 2 we have the supreme non-negotiables: birth and death. In practice, even when births are 'planned', there are multitudes of imponderables. Even in suicides, a combination of unwanted and uncontrolled circumstances will have led to that sad point. The overall rhythm of birth and death is also seen in nature: 'a time to plant and a time to uproot'. This is the ordered universe where everything has a pattern. That pattern can also be seen in communal relationships and in the whole fabric of human society (v. 3).

Human emotions

The rhythms of life do not continue without emotions being aroused. Joy and sorrow are inseparable from lives that are rounded by the basic facts of life and death, and will often be expressed in the physical actions of mourning and dancing (v. 4). It is probably within this basic realm of human emotions that we are to understand the puzzling expression about scattering and gathering stones (v. 5). Some have seen it as a reference to demolishing an old building and building a new one, or to removing stones from a field to make it productive. Probably it refers to amicable and aggressive relationships in nations and communities, while the reference to 'embracing' makes the same point in individual terms. Relationships have both positive and negative aspects, and confrontation as well as conciliation is a necessary part of human affairs.

Possessions

We live in a material world and our author reminds us of the nature of possessions (v. 6). We must not cultivate a world-rejecting asceticism; there is a time to 'search' and to 'keep'. Nor must we become totally wrapped up in possessions; there is a time to 'give up' and 'throw away'. Here we have neatly encapsulated the Bible's consistent attitude to the material world.

Creative and destructive

Turning to verse 7, 'tearing' may seem less attractive than 'mending', but there are times when wrong relationships have to be broken and perhaps a limb removed to save the whole body. Similarly, part of maturity is to know when to say something and when to say nothing. Hatred and war (v. 8) may seem purely negative, but when we are faced with real evil bent on destruction, it is not part of godliness to fail to resist.

The overall theology of this passage is twofold. First, we learn the overarching providence of God in the bewildering array of human and material circumstances. We have no control over these, but God does, and we know that he understands the end from the beginning.

Second, we realize that life has its mysteries and that we need wisdom to seize our opportunities and to know how to act in different circumstances. Here again, the great biblical doctrine of the interplay of God's providence and human responsibility is at the heart of the passage.

PRAYER

Lord, help us to trust you in the bad times
and praise you at all times.

ETERNITY IN OUR HEARTS

The beautiful words of verses 1–8 are interrupted by verse 9, which could have come straight from chapter 1. Whether life brings us all we desire or whether we feel cheated, what does it matter in the long run? In a Job-like expression, *Qoheleth* sees this burden as inflicted by God himself (v. 10). What if we are simple playthings tossed on the ocean and subject to a remote God who cares nothing for us? The problem of futility remains.

God's inscrutable wisdom

Our author's comment is that, by arranging a time for everything, God's activity can be described as 'beautiful' (v. 11). This means more than 'appropriate'; it has overtones of the 'good' in the creation stories in Genesis 1 and 2. What God does reflects his own beauty and order and fulfils his ultimate purposes. Thus, although we cannot see the whole picture, we can be certain that there is a pattern and that it is lovely and ultimately good.

The fact that humans are in God's image means that they have 'eternity' in their hearts. This is further defined in verse 14: 'everything God does will endure for ever'. This is the root of both our security and our sense of mystery and bafflement. 'They cannot fathom what God has done from beginning to end' (v. 11). We are aware that we have come from God and we return to him, but in between we often feel lost and afraid.

How do we respond?

Verses 12 and 13 make up the first of two short sections beginning with 'I know', where Mr Preacher again reflects on how his theology works out in daily life. Eating, drinking and work (or, if you like, leisure and business), which can be so wearisome, can partake of a deeper significance when seen as the gift of God. Without such significance, they become part of the grinding routine. Again, this fits in with the overall picture of God and the material world that runs through the Bible. God created the world and it was 'good'; because of the Fall it was spoilt, but one day God will bring in a new creation. Meanwhile, there are still glimpses of goodness that recall Eden and anticipate heaven. A good meal enjoyed with loved ones, a drink and a chat, work that stimulates and stretches, these are all good gifts and part of the fabric of life. When seen from the perspective of God's sovereignty, we can rejoice and find in them anticipations of the life to come.

But does it lead anywhere?

The second 'I know' (v. 14) affirms that what God does lasts, and that he has no external restraints preventing him from doing exactly what he plans. This leads to reverential fear, the atmosphere of worship in which life can be lived without ending in a sense of futility. God, not humans, is in charge of the cycle of life and he sees and oversees the entire course of events.

Verse 15 returns to the theme of 1:9–11 and, in other words, asserts that 'there is nothing new under the sun'. But there is a significant difference in the final phrase: 'God will call the past into account.' Nothing, then, is insignificant, because God watches over it with his all-seeing eye. The phrase is difficult and can mean 'God calls back the past', but in any case it means that every moment is significant and thus not meaningless.

Human ingenuity and effort cannot by themselves adequately assess the significance of time. The author does not use the word 'faith', but that is the realm in which he is moving. The world he maps out in chapter 3 is no different from that of chapter 1, but the addition of God and the reality of judgment give the scene a different perspective. When I lived in Durham, I worked in St Johns College, which lay under the shadow of the cathedral. The medieval street in which it stood was characterful but could also be claustrophobic. However, if you climbed to the top of the cathedral, there spread in front of you was a magnificent panorama of Durham city and much of the surrounding countryside. You could still see the college and the street but as part of a whole wider context. So here, Mr Preacher invites us to look at the daily scene in a wider setting. Huge problems remain. He will not shirk these, but a new perspective has been introduced.

REFLECTION

Augustine said, 'O God, you have made us for yourself, and our hearts are restless until they find rest in you.'

THERE IS JUDGMENT

A new issue emerges. If God will judge, why does he not judge now? The news is full of disaster and tragedy, from the murders of children to devastating earthquakes, and yet God appears inactive. Often there is corruption, discrimination and favouritism in the 'place of judgment' and the 'place of justice' (v. 16).

God's timescale

In a remarkable verse, Mr Preacher states important truths about God's judgment. Firstly, it is not arbitrary: it deals with 'both the righteous and the wicked' (v. 17). This again is at the heart of biblical theology. Psalm 73:17 speaks of being in God's sanctuary and understanding that the final destinies of the righteous and wicked are different. Secondly, this judgment proceeds according to a divine rather than human timescale. Humans are not gods; only God knows and controls times and seasons.

No false superiority

This prevents an unreasonable arrogance and acts as a reminder that, to all outward appearances, we are no better off than the animals that share the planet with us. In particular, we all die. Is that the end of the story? If verse 18 sounds like negative and despairing cynicism, we must notice the words, 'so that they may see'. God is not acting arbitrarily; rather he is demonstrating that the injustices of life show that we cannot discern our destiny any more than the animals can. Our fallenness, part of which is an 'under the sun' perspective, blinds us to our true nature.

The universal death of living creatures in an undeniable fact. In that respect, humans have no immunity or superiority; in that respect, the old meaninglessness returns. In moments of bereavement, disillusionment and melancholia, verse 19 expresses clearly and starkly what the world looks like. Verse 20 echoes Genesis 3:19 and reminds us that we are made of the same material as the world in general. We all go to *Sheol*, the world of the dead.

Verse 21 may be a question, as the NIV takes it, or it may be a statement, but in any case a new idea is introduced—that of destiny after death. The ambiguity may be deliberate; what happens after death is not open to observation, and no conclusions about final destiny can be drawn simply by observing a corpse.

Enjoy your work

Even if the future is unknown, it is important to engage fully in our responsibilities and, indeed, to enjoy them. The last part of verse 22 does not refer to eternal destiny but to what is to come in our earthly lives. What we do on earth has value even though we cannot tell what it is.

This chapter is both profound and poetic, rooted deeply in the theology of the creation narratives. Whatever else the seven days of creation mean, they certainly affirm that God created time as the context in which life is to be lived. The beautiful reflection in these verses on the providence that governs times and seasons is a celebration of God's ceaseless care for all the bewildering variety of life.

If we ignore the reality of death and simply treat time as a succession of moments, though, we will end up disillusioned. On the other hand, if we see the fact of death as the only reality, we will cripple any achievement and end up in cynicism and despair. The author has emphasized that God gives life and that there is a sphere beyond life where the external significance of all that has been done will be assessed. This gives to everything a significance beyond itself and is an important reminder that many apparent failures and unfinished projects have not yet been finally judged.

In these first three chapters, Mr Preacher has presented a problem: the fundamental meaninglessness of the universe and life in it. From 2:24 to the end of chapter 3, however, he introduces God and hints at a solution, without developing it at this point. If the perspective is wholly 'under the sun' then despair is going to be inevitable. Our author will not allow us to jump to easy and quick solutions; we must feel the sheer weight of the problem before we can appreciate the solution.

REFLECTION

Time is a gift, not a right or a burden. Let us use what we have wisely and well.

NO RESPITE

Mr Preacher has laid out his stall, and from chapter 4 to 10 we will explore further various aspects of life 'under the sun'. The style often resembles the book of Proverbs, with vivid word-pictures encapsulating a person or situation. It is not always easy to follow the flow of thought but, again like Proverbs, groups of sayings occur that relate to particular themes. Each section faces huge issues and there is some overlap as topics are covered from different angles. Here, in chapter 4, the underlying theme of relationships binds the various topics together; the need for community and companionship is a note struck continually.

The destruction of relationships

Few things can be more destructive of true community than grinding oppression. Verses 1–3 do not refer to a particular regime but to all oppressive situations. The picture is grim: brutal totalitarianism, of which our world has still so many examples, has caused untold heartbreak. There are no 'comforters'; grief and oppression are desperately lonely conditions.

This leads to despair: death is better than life; indeed, not being born at all is better than both. Again the significant phrase 'under the sun' occurs; without God there is only hopelessness. This is all in contrast to 2:26 and 3:22, which describe life under the hand of God. Those passages must be held in tension with this one. The book of Ecclesiastes is exploring differing worldviews and giving vivid expression to both. At times, one will appear more real than the other. What is important is that the author is determined to explore ruthlessly the consequences of a worldview whose perspective is limited to what is 'under the sun'. Without God, there is simply no solution.

Envy is deadly

In the Western world, on the whole, we may mercifully be free from the kind of oppression outlined in verses 1–3, but we would be wrong to imagine that it has no relevance for us. Mr Preacher now goes on to demonstrate how relationships are destroyed by envy, by competition gone mad. This leads to another type of oppression:

a trampling on others to get to the top, a back-stabbing and back-biting culture and an ever more frantic rat race. Again the end result is emptiness.

The answer cannot simply be to opt out, however: 'The fool folds his hands' (v. 5). Folded hands are a metaphor for idleness, and Proverbs 6:10–11 sees this as a sure road to poverty. The translation 'ruins himself' (NIV) is rather weak; literally the Hebrew phrase means 'eats his own flesh'. This vividly carries on the overall theme of destruction of relationships, for the idle one is ruining his relationship with himself.

A better way is advocated in verse 6. 'Two handfuls' suggests a grasping of as much as is possible, and in this context suggests excess. 'One handful' suggests that only part of our energies ought to go into work; it is not the whole of life. Excessive concentration on work ends up in the familiar cul-de-sac of chasing the wind.

Mr Preacher has stated important truths about work that flow ultimately from Genesis 2, where work is not seen as a curse or a burden. Adam is given the task of tending the garden (Genesis 2:15), while the vision of heaven in the last chapters of the Bible also includes work: 'His servants will serve him' (Revelation 22:3). What happens as a result of the Fall is that work becomes associated with frustration and exhaustion (Genesis 3:19).

Work is a vital part of our lives, and one of the great anomalies of our society is that many people can find no work while others are ground down by the relentless pressures of ever-busier schedules. Our author focuses here on the discord. The fallen world finds both idleness and excessive busyness a disillusionment. The temptation is to over-react and become a slave either to hedonism or to frenetic activism. Neither holds the key to happiness or a secure society. The essentially self-centred nature of both extremes leads to broken relationships and to the oppression already outlined. If our centre of gravity is ourselves, and if we have the power to do so, we will inevitably oppress those under us. The extremes mentioned are both examples of the 'envy' of which *Qoheleth* speaks.

PRAYER

Lord, bless our work and cause it to prosper, but help us not to make it the centre of our lives. Amen.

Two Are Better Than One

The theme of loneliness and companionship, and their relationship to work, continues in this section. Our author is particularly concerned about two things: the solitary person who has no one to help (vv. 7–12), and the frustrations of power and its succession.

A man all alone

Verses 7–8 present a sad picture of an individual with no friends or relatives. No reason is given; we do not know if this is a result of choice or of misfortune. Whatever the reason, for this man, life has simply become a long grind devoted entirely to work. This again raises the deeper question of the point and purpose of living. Once again, if this is viewed from the perspective of 'under the sun', there is no answer. At this stage, Mr Preacher simply outlines the problem.

The blessing of companionship

In some respects, companionship is the answer to the situation of verses 7–8. The statement that 'two are better than one' (v. 9) is pragmatic. Both the general statement that their work is more satisfactory and the three illustrations given are utilitarian rather than exploring the general benefits of companionship. The first illustration is probably of falling into a pit, but also refers to misfortunes more generally. The second may refer to marriage, but perhaps also to huddling together for warmth in a hostile world. The third is enigmatic and may refer to a lonely traveller attacked by bandits. The 'threefold cord' is a powerful expression, common in the ancient world. It also occurs in the Epic of Gilgamesh, which is about a ruler of Erech or Uruk (Genesis 10:10) on the north bank of the Euphrates. It tells the story of two friends who team up against overwhelming odds and whose companionship provides a 'third cord'. Some have also detected a reference to a son born to a married couple.

There is little comfort here in this bleak pragmatism. Mr Preacher says nothing about how such companions may be found, nor does he raise the possibility that companions may turn out to be fickle or treacherous. He is forcing us to face up to the problems of work, whether alone or together.

No hope in promotion

Verses 13–16 give another snapshot of the dangers of isolation and work, in the sense that they deal both with the difficulty of giving up and the folly of trying to please people. Many commentators have tried to identify the characters here but the scene is too general for such attempts to be convincing.

Wisdom is not guaranteed simply by years, and Mr Preacher contrasts the king who ought to have been wise with the humble youth who is wise, in spite of all disadvantages. All the king's achievements, whatever they may have been, fade before the rising star of this youth. Yet, in turn, the youth's popularity wanes and there is no lasting substance to his reputation. This is yet another example of the book's basic thesis that everything is meaningless.

Work and companionship are both great blessings, but 'under the sun' neither lasts, nor do they change the essential meaninglessness of life. This is the world of the Fall, where all good things have an inbuilt bias to go wrong.

The author uses every device—proverb, anecdote, repetition and irony—to carry the theme forward. He wants to make sure that the problem is explored from all angles and that all false solutions and evasions are shown for what they are. The material is arranged thematically rather than logically. This, in itself, reflects the 'meaninglessness' of life 'under the sun'. Our experiences do not follow a logical pattern and often there seems to be little sense in what happens.

Mr Preacher will not let us off the hook; chapter 4 ends with another declaration of meaninglessness, and we are conscious that we still have a long way to travel. Again we are reminded of the world of Genesis 1—11 where the Fall brings alienation, first for Adam and Eve and then for Cain and Abel, and Noah. At the same time, the problems of relationships and loneliness dealt with here are highly contemporary ones. So much misery is caused by broken relationships and so much more by loneliness.

A chapter like this does not give any answers to these problems, but it is a painful, if necessary, way of reminding us of the inadequacy of our human resources.

PRAYER

Lord, we bring you our failures in relationship and our loneliness and ask that in you we may find healing for both. Amen.

The FEAR of the LORD

Our author, having shown us the sheer grind and unremitting toil of so much of human life, now forcibly reminds us of a world that is not confined to 'under the sun'. He is not going off at a tangent; he has been concerned with human relationships and now he turns to a yet more important relationship, that with God. Much of what is said here focuses on the importance of authenticity and of speaking with integrity.

The approach to God

Verse 1 gives us the only mention in the book of 'the house of God', and almost certainly the temple is meant. However, the specific reference is less important than what is being said about the approach to God. Even before we arrive, there is preparation—'guard your steps'— which suggests both reverence and expectancy. There is always the danger of a casual and frivolous approach to God. 'Listen' has its full biblical sense of absorbing and acting upon what is heard, rather than simply being present when words are spoken. Careless, empty words are an affront to God and should be avoided. Mr Preacher sees hasty and thoughtless words as an offering that only a fool could make. Empty words are the language of an empty heart.

The reason for such caution is that there is a vast difference between God and us. The fact that God is 'in heaven' (v. 2) does not mean that he is not on earth, rather that he is glorious beyond our understanding. This is the transcendent God so eloquently portrayed in passages such as Genesis 1, Isaiah 40 and Job 38. There is no point in trying to deceive or manipulate this God, as he is utterly beyond our understanding.

Empty words

It is not entirely clear why there is a reference to dreams in verse 3, but both dreams and empty words deal in fantasies. What Mr Preacher wants is for all our relationships, especially the one with God, to be authentic. Authentic prayer is not likely to be wordy. Indeed, Jesus warns against this in Matthew 6:7: 'And when you pray, do not keep on babbling like pagans, for they think they will be heard because of their many words.' Instead, it holds a sense of the awesomeness of God and the reverence due to him. Prayer is a test of how genuine our relationship with God is. Instead of a stream of pious phrases, it is a serious engagement with the Lord Almighty.

Dangerous vows

A vow is a particular type of speaking that demands total honesty (v. 4). Vows were an important aspect of ancient Israel's worship of God and were not to be made hastily (Proverbs 20:25); they could be an expression of devotion to God (Psalm 22:25) or an action carried out in return for God's blessing (Numbers 21:1–3). Here in Ecclesiastes, the emphasis is on avoiding procrastination, which is seen as a mark of the fool. While verse 5 is an important reminder of the voluntary nature of vows, we should remember that if they are made they set up a solemn agreement with God, who takes them seriously and regards them as binding.

This goes to the heart of what worship is about. There is a real danger of pouring out words when our hearts and minds are somewhere else. That is why the reference to dreams recurs in verse 7. Much of what passes as worship is often daydreaming. We are familiar with the experience of being in church and going through the motions while our minds are on lunch, a problem at work, a journey we are about to make and so on. Sometimes we say words and sing songs which are, in effect, vows, but we forget them when we leave the service and may make all kinds of excuses to evade what we have said.

The remedy for this kind of mindless babble is to 'stand in awe of God' (v. 7). This anticipates the end of the book (12:13), where the fear of God is seen as central to human life and where the right use of words is emphasized. Standing in awe of God is at the very heart of the Wisdom tradition (see, for example, the poem in Job 28). It is a view of God which treats him with caution and respect and recognizes that worship involves treading on holy ground.

All of this means that entering the presence of God requires careful preparation; we do not simply rush in. It requires silence, reverence and a teachable, humble heart and mind. This is the way to real and authentic living.

REFLECTION

Meditate on the words of Jesus: 'God is spirit, and his worshippers must worship in spirit and truth' (John 4:24).

The TROUBLE *with* MONEY

Mr Preacher returns to the theme of power and relationships, and here they are particularly entangled with money. For many, wealth is seen as a panacea, but our author dismisses that view. He gives a number of reasons for this, and then again hints at a solution at the end of the chapter.

The tyranny of bureaucracy

In verses 8–9 we have a marvellous, penetrating picture of hierarchy and its debilitating effects. Here economic disparity is worked into the system and a network of corruption operates with impunity, reaching to the top. The social system with its endless evasions and delays, its institutionalized buck-passing, is relentlessly pilloried. In the end, only those at the top profit. The land is the source of prosperity in this society, and the poor have no stake in that prosperity. In a viewpoint restricted to life 'under the sun', there is simply no remedy.

The trouble with money

Money is a craving that can never be satisfied, for it simply leads to further craving (v. 10). This is the burden of 1 Timothy 6:10: 'the love of money is a root of all kinds of evil.' Such desire becomes a ravening monster, devouring everything that is wholesome and creating, instead of fulfilment, a new and devastating experience of meaninglessness. Verse 11 is a cutting indictment of the consumer society. Wealth tends to lead to hoarding rather than using, and in the end becomes no more than a drug and a curse. Indeed, it leads to insomnia as people worry about their wealth and its security. By contrast, those who work hard sleep well, even though they may be poor (v. 12).

Nothing to show for it

In verses 13–17 we have a worst-case scenario. Wealth, whether carefully hoarded or lost through disaster or carelessness, is fickle and no respecter of persons. Humans leave this life exactly as they entered it: with nothing. Wealth has no enduring significance. Like the rich man in Luke 12:13–21, immense riches are simply left behind, and there is a sour sense of frustration. If life does not take wealth away, then death will. Verse 17 is one of the bleakest in the book. Words such as 'darkness', 'affliction' and 'anger' show a total disillusionment and a nihilistic view of the world.

Back to God

The bleakness of verses 8–17 is notable for its lack of mention of God, but now he appears four times in three verses (vv. 18–20). There is a reality greater than that experienced 'under the sun'. This little section shows how wisdom lies in accepting food, drink and work as gifts from God. They become destructive forces when allowed to dominate, but are good and wholesome if received from God. 'Eating' and 'drinking' express contentment, fellowship and peace and stand for all the small yet satisfying pleasures of ordinary living. Not all wealth is wrong; indeed, when given by God and stewarded as a gift from him it is a great blessing. Such an attitude will free people from vain speculations on the outcome of matters over which they have no control. God is at work in all of life, not only in the spiritual 'highs' but in the everyday business of living.

This chapter, while ostensibly about wealth, is ultimately about attitudes. The difference lies in how we see the simple satisfactions found in our world. If our horizons are bounded by this life and its rewards, we shall do anything to be wealthy (hence the popularity of lotteries). However, if we see life itself and the pleasures it brings as gifts from God, our whole outlook is changed and we cease to be obsessed with possessions.

Chapter 3:11 speaks of God putting eternity into people's hearts. If that is the case, then nothing less than God himself can satisfy. As humans, though, we are fickle and easily distracted from our true destiny. Thus Mr Preacher is determined to show us again and again how all other roads lead to dead ends. We still have quite a way to go and other blind alleys to follow, but the echoes of another country, like music breaking through from another channel as we listen to the radio, prevent us from becoming too settled in the world 'under the sun'.

PRAYER

Lord, teach us true priorities and make us thankful for all the gifts you have given us. Amen.

Who Can Tell?

The theme of money and possessions continues in this chapter, but the more fundamental issues of the unknowability of the future and the elusiveness of satisfaction are an undercurrent throughout. This underlines the lessons learned in chapters 4 and 5 and points forward to the further reflections on destiny in the following chapters.

Inability to enjoy life

In verses 1–6 we have again the mystery of providence (explored in chapter 3). God does indeed give generously (all the gifts and riches of chapter 2) but he does not force upon us the ability to enjoy them. This may seem capricious and unfair, but it is important to note that there is no suggestion that the person described here recognizes and acknowledges God as the source of the gifts, or indeed that he recognizes them as gifts at all. Again this is the viewpoint from 'under the sun'.

As with possessions, so with family. Many of the Psalms (for example, 127 and 128) speak of the blessings of a large family, but here only negative aspects are emphasized. Failure to enjoy life and to have a decent burial at the end is worse than not having lived at all. To be spared the misery of consciousness seems preferable to the tedium and emptiness of life 'under the sun'. Long life is merely a greater opportunity for misery.

Unsatisfied cravings

Human appetite is ravenous and indeed has the insatiability of death itself (v. 7). Israel's Canaanite neighbours told of Mot, the god of death, whose jaws stretched from heaven to earth and devoured everything in their way. This appetite is as much a characteristic of the 'wise' as of the 'foolish'. In our fallen world, ravenous desire is a reality and we have to learn how to come to terms with it. The only way to do so is to be satisfied with 'what the eye sees' (v. 9): being content with where God has placed us and what he has given us. This calls for a fundamental change of attitude and priorities. Contentment is not related to our wealth or status but to our desires, which are ultimately governed by ourselves or by God.

Who knows what is good?

Mr Preacher has reached something of an impasse here and he speaks of the basic impossibility of understanding what life is about. Verse 10 describes the fixed destiny of everything and everyone. To name someone is to denote character and destiny. In Genesis 32:28 God gives Jacob the new name Israel and thus indicates a new future for him. Humans, tied to life 'under the sun', have already had bounds set for them and they cannot contend with God, who is the stronger one, as Job realized (Job 9:1–12). Words, as in 5:2, can simply cloud the issue, their quantity trying to compensate for their lack of substance (v. 11). What is needed is some perspective that will set human life in a wider context and explore its abiding significance. The future remains a mystery, and no inner resources or external inquiry will unravel that enigma.

Mr Preacher has brought us to a locked door; we do not know what is beyond it and we do not have the key. Yet verse 10 gives us hints of something beyond ('one who is stronger than he') as we reflect on his penetrating analysis of human striving and ignorance. The mystery of providence and the impossibility of contending with God can be seen in a different light than is found here: see Psalm 139, where the psalmist finds it a true and lasting sense of security.

Words may be empty, but these verses in Ecclesiastes must be balanced with other biblical passages about the effectiveness of words, not least what is said in 12:11. After all, *Qoheleth* himself is using words to great effect to force us to face up to reality. His words are most certainly not unprofitable; they are hard, but they force us to confront fundamental issues.

This chapter forces us to face up to the fact that we are weak and vulnerable. Knowing that God is stronger than us should not crush us, however, but can lead us to a true attitude of wisdom and sense of our own vulnerability. We must not look to money, favourable circumstances or anything other than God to be the true foundation on which we build our lives.

REFLECTION

A chapter like this makes uncomfortable reading, but it is not intended to drive us to despair. It can help us to adjust our priorities, so that we will rest in God himself.

PARADOX *upon* PARADOX

The style of this chapter is dominated by proverbs, and especially proverbs that embody paradoxes. Mr Preacher is intent on making us think, and this rhetorical technique does just that. Basic issues of wisdom bearing especially on adversity, evil and ultimate meaning are explored.

When life is tough

Death is the great arbiter; questions of reputation and significance are decided not at the beginning but at the end. A dirge is more profound than a cheery song because it opens eyes to the reality. This is also the emphasis in Psalm 90:12: 'Teach us to number our days aright, that we may gain a heart of wisdom.' Occasions of festivity do not have the same power to make us think seriously on what life is about. *Qoheleth* has praised the pleasures of life often enough, but here he is concerned with the fact that we are mortal and that we must come to terms with death. Only then can we live fully. Our attitude to death is closely related to the kind of people we are in our innermost selves. A 'name' (v. 1) is more than a label; it is our fundamental character, and that is what ultimately shapes our destiny.

The 'heart' (vv. 3–4) is the centre of the human personality, and the wise, whatever they may be on the surface, are always fully aware of the great issues of life and death. Verses 5 and 6 relate this awareness to wise and foolish behaviour, particularly in the astringency of a sharp but ultimately helpful piece of advice and the superficiality of empty laughter. Such laughter is yet another example of the meaninglessness that marks the perspective of those whose horizons are limited to life 'under the sun'.

Pitfalls to avoid

Mr Preacher is realistic; however much he may praise adversity, he recognizes that there are dangers to which we must be alert. Verse 7 is more closely related to verses 1–6 than it first appears. Verses 1–6 have spoken of the inner integrity brought by facing up to the issues of life and death; here in verse 7 are two ways in which that integrity can be destroyed. The first is extortion and oppression, which can destroy people's spirits, and the second is bribery, which corrupts life into a mere pursuit of gain.

Qoheleth then turns to the virtue of patience, the taking of the long view (v. 8). He warns against making hasty decisions, before the whole course of action is plain. This is a particular warning to our society, so dominated as we are with fads and fashions. A related issue is the tendency to sudden bursts of anger (v. 9), which again fails the challenge to be patient and wait for a better outcome.

Nostalgia is a particular example of the foolishness of not waiting for the final outcome of life. Pining for years gone by is a sure way to avoid the opportunities of the present, but it is a seductive temptation. Often, in the church, we can cling to old ways of doing things or long for some mythical past. Trying to freeze a particular moment and live there is another way of avoiding 'the end of a matter' (v. 8), and it only destroys the future outlook that is at the heart of the gospel.

We need wisdom

We cannot live in the past but, like a legacy or inheritance, wisdom can help us to live in the present (v. 11). This is a mundane view of wisdom, more concerned with practicalities than with deeper issues, but it does not mean that both wisdom and money should be despised. Used wisely, as gifts of God, they are a blessing.

Wisdom in the Old Testament is many-faceted and covers the whole of life. The book of Proverbs especially illustrates this with its profound picture of Wisdom and creation in chapter 8. The paradoxical idea of death being better than life gives a completely new slant on the present. Since death will provide the final verdict, then it becomes of great importance to make sure, in the present, that the verdict is a favourable one. Moreover, this provides true wisdom for all of life's phases and for the lesser 'death' represented by the end of each phase. The New Testament gives a fuller content to life in the 'in-between times', with its perspective of the 'now' and the 'not yet'. Such a view both helps us to have a certain detachment from what is fleeting and yet to value everyday life for its gifts and opportunities, which will all become part of the final assessment.

PRAYER

Lord, help us to live wisely, neither despising the present world nor thinking that it is the whole reality. Amen.

DISCOVERING *the* SCHEME *of* THINGS

Verses 13 and 14 introduce further reflections on wisdom and the context in which it operates. The theology here compares with the statement in Isaiah 45:7, 'I [Yahweh] bring prosperity and create disaster.' Jewish thinking has no place for dualism—the view that the universe is balanced between two roughly equal powers of good and evil. Wisdom will prevent us from engaging in too much speculation: there are many things we do not and cannot know, and it is wise for us to recognize our limitations. Life is not controlled by blind fate; nor is God capricious. Two great classic statements of this belief are those of Joseph: 'You intended to harm me, but God intended it for good' (Genesis 50:20); and of Paul: 'In all things God works for the good of those who love him' (Romans 8:28). Good times lead to happiness and bad times lead to the kind of serious thinking already advocated in the first part of the chapter. Wisdom helps us to see the value and the God-givenness of both these experiences.

Avoid presumption

Mr Preacher is continually presenting balance and perspective on all the issues he raises. God is indeed in control, but that does not prevent us from experiencing the anomalies of life in a particularly unpleasant way. Verse 15 is one of the contradictions that believers have felt in all ages, which is particularly explored in Psalm 73. Similarly, the book of Job shows us that the righteous suffer, and we all know examples of how the wicked and arrogant seem to prosper and are not, at least on earth, called to account. There are no concessions to modern-day prosperity teaching here: the life of faith may involve poverty, persecution and suffering.

Verses 16–18 should not be taken as a call to bland and anaemic moderation. We must notice first the irony of verse 16. In verse 20 the preacher states that no one is righteous, and this shows that verse 16 refers to a person's exaggerated sense of their own virtue. Some Christians still fall into this trap; some collapse the life of faith into rules and regulations that lead to an intense and inhibited lifestyle. Some frown on all enjoyment, however innocent. Similarly, the claim to excessive wisdom contains the idea of play-acting and posing as someone who has 'seen it all before'. The answer to this is not to fall into the opposite extreme of over-indulgence, which is the mark of the fool. The answer to both is the fear of God (v. 18), which will make us conscious both of our limitations and the remedy for them.

Wisdom is a source of strength that enables us to live well in the midst of dangers. It will ultimately have more value than the collective advice of city councils, which might simply produce outward conformity without inner resources. A word of caution in verse 20 sums up what the author has been saying: true righteousness, both in the sense of positive virtue and negative avoidance of sin, is unknown among humans. A particular example of human unright-eousness is loose, unkind and unreliable speech (vv. 21–22); see James 3:2 for a similar emphasis. Our own hearts and experiences echo the unkindness we often receive from others, and both show the unwise and perverse behaviour of human beings.

Wisdom is elusive

Qoheleth has been exploring wisdom from many angles, and, like the author of Job 28, has found it to be elusive. He wants to discover the meaning of the universe and whether there is a pattern behind the apparently pointless rhythms he has expounded so eloquently in chapter 1. In particular, he wants to understand the apparently relent-less wickedness and stupidity of humankind. First he speaks of a particular kind of woman (v. 26). This is not misogyny; rather it is a comment on how unwise love can ruin lives and cause distress—unless God takes a hand.

This is part of a general failure to live wisely, and here *Qoheleth* is speaking of his own experiences. His further comment on the sexes (v. 28) is not a universal truth but rather a wry remark on his failure to find wise living. The failure of both sexes is all but total.

His conclusion in verse 29 is that human lack of wisdom is funda-mentally to be traced to perversity. We are again in the world of Genesis 1—3, the world of original goodness, blighted by sin and rebellion. Ultimately this cannot be blamed on God, who 'made mankind upright' (v. 29).

REFLECTION

In Christ, the Wisdom of God, and with his forgiveness,
life can be remade and lived as God intended.

COPING *with* AUTHORITY

Chapter 8 continues the theme of the elusiveness of wisdom, particularly in relation to authority and justice. Again there are hints of an ultimate solution.

Verse 1 is taken by some commentators as the end of the previous section. It is probably better seen as an introduction to this section, referring to behaviour in a royal court. Wisdom, in the sense of understanding the 'explanation of things', is now to be applied to problems of authority and justice. It is God who makes the face shine (Exodus 34:29–30) and this is one of the hints of an ultimate solution that runs through the book.

Obeying the king

The Bible has much to say about authority, and especially about godly rule (see David's words in 2 Samuel 23:2–7). It is also realistic about tyrannical rule and condemns oppression. Romans 13:1–7 speaks of government as ordained by God for the ordering of society and to enable human beings to live together in reasonable harmony. Ecclesiastes 8:2–4 is a very pragmatic passage; *Qoheleth* is not concerned here with the philosophy of kingship but with the practical issues of how to behave wisely in a society where the king's word is law. Another good illustration of how to live effectively under this kind of totalitarian regime can be found in the book of Esther (see commentary).

The author again wants us to be realistic. Since the king's power is absolute, we need a strategy for survival. This is more than mere pragmatism, however. The passage is controlled by verse 2: 'you took an oath before God'. Ultimately the power of kings, like everything else, is under the sovereignty of God. Moreover, the obedience given to them will be, for the wise, governed by the 'proper time and procedure' (v. 5). This echoes chapter 3 and is a reminder that no king's power lasts for ever.

Authority has its limitations

No king, however powerful, has any control over the future (v. 8). This introduces a reflection on further limitations, not simply on all humans, but especially on those who exercise power. 'No one has power over the wind' (which means, in context, the spirit). It is impossible to confine the human spirit and no one can control someone's inner life. Further, no one can control death. Suicide seems an exception; yet even there, intolerable pressures have driven someone to take their own life and in that sense they have no control. War, also, is no respecter of persons; nor does wickedness release those captured in its clutches (v. 8).

The question of authority is a perplexing one and can often add to the sense of injustice and the futility of life, yet no human authority is absolute. *Qoheleth* is not giving us a solution; rather, with characteristic ambivalence he is showing how the mystery and uncertainty of life, while trying, is also a curb on despots and tyrants. More especially, death simply erects a frontier post that no human power can pass. Likewise, the depths of the human spirit and the mysteries of the future cannot be controlled or even predicted. This creates a total equality in face of the unknown and of death. Thus, although simply by observation we cannot tell what lies beyond, the very limitation of human power shows that there are mysteries which the most powerful and the most intelligent cannot fathom.

Kings and authorities do not have the final word. However much they may strut and fret their hour upon the stage, they are not of ultimate significance. Pragmatically, they are of great importance in the ordering of society, but in the eternal perspective they do not have lasting importance. Some parts of the Bible, notably Judges, speak of the descent into anarchy in a land where there is no king: 'In those days Israel had no king; everyone did as he saw fit' (Judges 21:25). All this is a reminder that a perspective limited to 'under the sun' will find no answer to the problem of authority, nor indeed anything else.

PRAYER

Lord, in this world of many competing authorities,
help us to live as responsible citizens but to give our
ultimate allegiance only to you. Amen.

COPING *with* ANOMALIES

Verse 9 is another bridging text, which glances back at the previous section and then goes on to consider the wider question of anomalies of injustice and misfortune.

Injustices and delays

Public recognition has little to do with real merit. Mr Preacher uses words that emphasize the care and thoroughness of his investigations. They were comprehensive—'all this'; they were observed—'I saw'; and they were the result of careful thought—'I applied my mind' (v. 9). After the general statement of the damaging effects of power (damaging, that is, to those who wield it) comes the difficult verse 10. The wicked are buried: the implication is that they get more than they deserve because they had acted in a disgraceful way in the holy place, probably Jerusalem. This is another example of the unrighteous prospering.

This injustice is further illustrated in the delay that often happens in offenders being brought to book (v. 11). A similar idea occurs in 2 Peter 3:3–4, where the author complains that everything continues as it did and 'scoffers' are not brought to judgment. Here in Ecclesiastes, the human problem, as so often in the Bible, is traced to the heart. The problem is not merely outward sins; human action is corrupted at its source.

There is an answer, however, and *Qoheleth* gives it positively in verse 12 and negatively in verse 13. He now spells out his belief that 'it will go better with God-fearing people'. Once again the repetition of 'God' shows how seriously he is opening the possibility of a perspective beyond this world and of judgment (not to be made explicit until chapter 12).

Not yet the final answer

The enigmas are real enough in the present. The phrase 'that occurs on earth' (v. 14) reminds us that, whatever may happen in the future, we are still in this world with all its unfairness, where virtue is punished and sin rewarded. We may have faith and glimpses of better things but the harsh realities of daily life remain. Once again, *Qoheleth* recommends taking simple pleasures such as eating, drinking and working as gifts from God (v. 15). This may show itself in simple ways: always saying grace before meals, thanking God that we have work to do rather than endlessly complaining about it, and looking for all the other gifts that God has scattered throughout our lives. Furthermore, verse 15 implies the importance of good rhythms of resting and working and the value of thanksgiving and gratitude.

None of this resolves the enigma; the deep mysteries of life remain. We have partial answers but they amount to a fragmentary picture. Indeed, trying to know too much leads to sleeplessness and frustration (v. 16). Any worldview that claims to capture the meaning of everything is a vain hope, empty words. This must, in the wise, produce a spirit of humility.

At the same time, we must not ignore the important phrase in verse 17, 'then I saw all that God has done'. Our ignorance is part of what it means to be human. We are created, we are fallen and our knowledge is not like that of God. The earlier part of the chapter spoke of authority and now here is the supreme authority. In Genesis 3:4–7, the desire to know everything ('good and evil') led to the present sorry state. The fact that this is what 'God has done' shows that there is a meaning, even if we cannot find it.

This suggests a different perspective. Humans are prone to arrogance and to claiming to 'know it all'. That way lies despair and death. Faith in God recognizes that while we cannot grasp all knowledge, we can know enough to live life well.

REFLECTION

Are our lives marked by gratitude or by continual complaining about inevitable difficulties and trials in our lives?

Sharing *a* Common Destiny

As *Qoheleth* continues his exploration of life, he deals with ultimate responses and the problems of a universe that does not seem to have moral coherence. He is grappling with the problem of life's overall meaning.

The obvious unfairness

In verses 1–6, Mr Preacher uses his characteristic style of observation, reflection and illustration. His concern is the common destiny of good and bad people and its apparently random nature, demonstrated by our total inability to foresee the future and make certain that we can carry out our plans and ideas. All of us have a chequered experience of life and all of us die, and there appears to be no overarching reason for it. Verse 2 catalogues a number of contrasts that carry echoes of other biblical language. 'Righteous' and 'wicked' are the common terms for our attitudes to God and our desire to obey or disobey him. 'Good' and 'sinful' are the result of such attitudes to God. 'Clean' and 'unclean' are terms referring to the holiness or otherwise of the people, and offering or failing to offer sacrifices is the visible expression of the inner condition of the heart. This is summed up at the end of the verse by a comment on oath-taking, which probably refers to loyalty to the covenant and embraces both belief and behaviour. The phrase 'in God's hands' (v. 1) is yet another reminder that there is more to life than can be explained by an 'under the sun' view.

For Mr Preacher, death is not just misfortune; it is an evil (v. 3). In earlier chapters he had floated the idea that death, and even not having been born at all, were preferable to living (4:2–3; 6:3–6), much as Job does (Job 3:16). Now, however, even mean and miserable living is considered better than being dead (v. 4). It is not that he is denying an afterlife; he is saying that what lies beyond death is shrouded in mystery. He again sounds a note of the total oblivion of the dead and how they are quickly forgotten, but again he is presenting the perspective 'under the sun' (v. 6). There is another realm, and in that realm there may be other answers. As far as this earthly life is concerned, however, death is final and irrevocable.

The appropriate action

In spite of this, Qoheleth is not advocating inertia. The word 'Go' in verse 7 is a summons to positive action. Life must not be allowed to pass by while we hope vaguely that something will happen; rather, we need positively to enjoy the gifts God gives us.

Life can be frittered away while we wait for an ideal moment to arrive. The good things of life, which were delusions when seen as absolutes, can and must be enjoyed when we accept them as signs of God's blessing. Food and wine, received from God's generous hands, are signs of his favour. In a hot climate, white clothes keep the wearer cool, and anointing with oil is like having a soak in a bubble bath (v. 8). Similarly, the joy of companionship in marriage is God's gift and also to be enjoyed. 'Meaningless days' (v. 9) reminds us that we cannot take any of these blessings for granted and that 'under the sun' we have no certainty.

Indeed, all must be undertaken positively and vigorously (v. 10) because Sheol will draw a line under all earthly activities. The fact that we know we will die is an incentive to make the most of the time given to us.

All this falls far short of a full vision of faith, but it is marked by vigorous realism. It both recognizes and insists on the certainty of death and the uncertainty of everything else, but refuses to use them as an excuse for hopelessness. It affirms the value of eating, drinking, loving and working and will have nothing to do with a bogus asceticism. Qoheleth does not believe in the 'prosperity gospel': he knows that godly living is no guarantee of avoiding hardship and tragedy. This is a healthy corrective to some of the more neurotic versions of living the Christian life, which are burdened with endless rules and regulations and are lacking in joy and vitality.

Life remains mysterious and apparently unfair and in that sense 'meaningless', yet it is full of God's gifts, including God-given opportunities that must be grasped. While this is not yet the full-orbed gospel, it is an important part of it.

PRAYER

Lord God, give us grateful hearts to receive your gifts with joy and use them wisely and well. Amen.

WISDOM ENDANGERED *but* VALUABLE

Wisdom cannot ultimately guarantee success in this world, but it remains valuable in spite of the vagaries of 'time and chance' (v. 11).

Time and chance

Even those who are endowed with great advantages may be thwarted by life. A good athlete may succumb to an illness or injury, a commander may fail to win a battle because of bad weather, a scholar may become bankrupt, and a politician can be discredited by the failure of his staff. Time, so eloquently evoked in chapter 3, changes situations and throws up unexpected chances or coincidences. Life has the unpredictability of a net or a trap for snaring prey (v. 12), and no one, however powerful or clever, can foresee the unexpected. All this is a powerful reminder of our vulnerability as humans and a warning not to try to pretend to a control we do not have. Life's frustrations remain real and, in particular, we do not know when death will come.

Public opinion is fickle

As so often, Mr Preacher illustrates his general point with a story (vv. 14–15). A poor wise man rescues a city from a far more powerful opponent and yet he is not remembered. An alternative, perhaps less likely interpretation is that the city was not saved because the wise man's advice was unheeded (v. 16). In any case, the emphasis is on the neglect of the poor man and his wisdom rather than the circumstances of the siege. The text includes difficulties, such as the identity of the 'poor man' (who some think is Mr Preacher himself), and the identification of the city, but the general outline is clever enough. Many attempts have been made to link the story with a specific historical incident, but none have commanded much support.

The conclusions that *Qoheleth* draws from this story are not wholly negative. He recognizes that wisdom can be shouted down or thwarted by superior strength, yet wisdom has an integrity and an enduring quality, which make it more worthy of respect than force or noise (v. 17). This means that while wisdom is subject to time and chance, they do not have the final word.

A number of observations follow from this. The first is that wisdom has moral connotations. It refers to far more than successful and resourceful living, neither of which are any guarantee of ultimate value. Wisdom, even when defeated, remains valuable, which strongly suggests that there is another realm of values where its true character will be seen.

Second, wisdom uses words in a judicious and persuasive manner (v. 17). Shouting and noise are associated with mindless bullying, and that is why, although apparently successful, force and coercion are morally bankrupt. Again this points to an arena other than public opinion where a different verdict will be given.

Third, although this chapter may appear profoundly pessimistic, even nihilistic, speaking of a life without ultimate purpose, this is not in fact the underlying meaning. The implications already noted, that this is not the final court of judgment, must govern our overall response to what is being said. Wisdom's voice is no less effective for its quietness. This enables the believer to keep going in an unpredictable and morally confused world, and to look for a verdict other than simply the one that makes the most noise.

The three references to God in the previous reading (9:1, 7, 9) underline the providential control of life seen in this chapter. This is the perspective of faith, and faith can discern divine overruling where observation and experience can see only frustration and inequality. This is a necessary basis for breaking out of the futility in which a perspective of 'under the sun' traps us. Qoheleth is determined to uncover everything about life under the sun before he gives us his conclusions in the final chapter.

As a powerful expression of both the frustrations of living and the perspective of faith, this chapter is masterly. There are no easy answers, no rush to happy endings and no evading of harsh realities. Faith and wisdom, in spite of their apparent weakness, are seen not only to hold their own but also to challenge the noisy consensus. Qoheleth shows robustness and astringency, which may be painful but are also invigorating and clarifying.

REFLECTION

Wisdom is not only valuable for its guidance in this world, but for its evidence that beyond is another realm of reality, where the full stature of wisdom will be realized.

FOLLY IS EVERYWHERE

With chapter 10 we reach the end of the long central section of the book (chs. 4—10). In chapters 9—10 he particularly focuses on ultimate responses and attitudes and the outcome of both wisdom and folly.

Character and choices

There is no real break between chapters 9 and 10: in proverbial style, verse 1 illustrates the truth of 9:15–18. The principle here is obvious throughout the whole of life. A tiny drop of poison will make a whole cup undrinkable; a small spillage will pollute a river; a tiny misplaced cog in an engine can bring a vehicle to an standstill; one act of infidelity can ruin a relationship.

Qoheleth goes on to talk about how this inclination to folly can be traced to the heart, which, in the Bible, is the inner nature that makes us what we are. 'Right' and 'left' (v. 2) have, of course, nothing to do with politics but rather reflect the ancient belief that the right hand was associated with power and competence, and the left with weakness and inability. This usage is still reflected in our words 'dexterity' and 'sinister'.

Folly is brash and draws attention to itself, and verse 3 conjures up all kinds of pictures of swaggering, loutish behaviour, rowdiness and embarrassingly public displays of stupidity. Verse 4, by contrast, speaks of a particular situation where 'calmness' rather than brash aggression can do wonders. Such loud behaviour will not impress authorities, and only the quiet demeanour of wisdom (9:17) will avail.

Folly in places of power

It would be wonderful if folly were absent from high places, but history, even up to the present day, shows that this is not so. Rulers (the word is of wide application) have great capacity to cause havoc, not least because of the frequent disparity between position and ability. Verses 6 and 7 sound odd in our egalitarian society, where we do not believe that a person's background should be an obstacle to their rising to positions of power and influence, but we must remember that in ancient society, only certain classes of people ever came to any position of power. Secondly, *Qoheleth* is speaking more of character and ability than of actual social position. However democratic we may be, we have to recognize that certain people do not have leadership qualities, and if such people are given high office the result will be disastrous. Mr Preacher simply uses the imagery of his time. 'Horseback' (v. 7) reflects the ancient world where horses were associated with kingship and wealthy lifestyle. In any case, the main thrust of this section is that folly should be a disqualification from leadership.

Pictures of folly

Qoheleth now gives us a series of proverbs illustrating the general theme of the consequences of folly. One type of folly is that of revenge and vindictiveness (v. 8)—and this may be a link with the previous section, for those in power have greater opportunities for malice.

It is not only malicious activities, however, that have inbuilt dangers. All of life has its perils, and verses 9–11 speak of some of them. Verses 9 and 10 are exquisitely balanced. Verse 9 warns that even good and productive activity may bring danger, yet the author is not encouraging a timid passivity, and in verse 10 he speaks of the painstaking nature of wisdom. The word translated 'skill' in the NIV is in fact 'wisdom'. Wisdom, unlike folly, is not brash and hasty but takes great pains and prepares well for the task. Yet wisdom will not spend so long in preparation that the task cannot be done, and this is the point of the little vignette of the uncharmed snake (v. 11).

Mr Preacher is warning of the danger of extremes. Wisdom is neither brash and hasty nor ultra-cautious. Moreover, wisdom discerns which situations need a lot of caution and which need swift action. In particular, wisdom is needed to prevent activities that are good in themselves from being spoilt or nullified by foolish and rash actions or by slothful cowardice.

REFLECTION

Think about your attitude to your work and life in general.
Have you been rash when you needed to pause, or have you
procrastinated instead of getting on with what needed to be done?

WORDS & ATTITUDES

Qoheleth has had much to say about words, as indeed all Wisdom literature does, and as he nears the end of this section he has still more to present on the subject.

Foolish words

Mr Preacher makes it very plain that it is not words as such that he is condemning. After all, words are his own trade, and he describes wise words as 'gracious', with all the connotations of blessing, kindness and positive help. How different, though, are the words of fools! Their words are destructive both of themselves and others. Foolish talk may begin with nonsense and buffoonery, but it ends with 'wicked madness' (v. 13). Moreover, the number of words used by fools is excessive (v. 14). They lack content and lead to ignorance rather than enlightenment.

The point of verse 14b is probably that the fool has no real knowledge of the present and is therefore a totally unreliable guide to the future. Wise people will always admit to agnosticism about the future and, if they do comment on it, their words will be shrewd and tentative. Words are always powerful, but in the mouths of fools that power is destructive. Not all words are foolish, but the endless comments on everything by the media are a good illustration of verse 14b. How often the lack of future knowledge has been demonstrated in confident media predictions: for example, when the Prime Minister will resign, who will be the next Archbishop, or even what the weather will be.

Foolish actions and attitudes

A fool is not shown up only by his words but also by his actions, because both spring up from fundamental attitudes. At root, the fool is lazy; Proverbs has many word-pictures of the sluggard who cannot get out of his bed and for whom no excuse to stop working is too pathetic (Proverbs 24:30–34; 26:13–16). Here the picture is similar: even the familiar world of work and daily landmarks is beyond the fool (v. 15).

As he sums up this section, *Qoheleth* applies the basic life choices of wisdom and folly to national life. The primary need for a country is to have a wise and mature leader. The word 'child' (v. 16, NIV footnote) refers not to calendar years but to maturity. In 1 Kings 3:7, Solomon recognizes the need for God-given wisdom to rescue him from being a 'child'. *Qoheleth* has often praised personal enjoyment, including eating and drinking, but in verse 16 he is speaking of drunken irresponsibility, such as, for example, the behaviour of the royal court in Esther 1. Verse 17 makes the same point in a positive sense. The contrast is not so much between youth and age as between responsibility and irresponsibility. The leaders of a nation must show a true balance in their rhythms of living so that examples are given of sensible behaviour rather than excess.

Verses 18–19 apply the same theme to the community and individual citizen. Verse 18 speaks of the self-destructive nature of folly. This is not so much divine judgment as the inherent decay of the 'house' that folly builds. We have a similar emphasis in the story of the wise and foolish builders who raised houses on rock and sand respectively (Matthew 7:24–27). Verse 19 powerfully and epigrammatically pillories the foolish life, which is totally limited to eating, drinking and spending money.

The chapter ends with a warning to be wise and discreet even in our inner thoughts and private places (v. 20). Attitudes have a habit of making themselves known, and there are always 'little birds' ready to tell of indiscretions and stupidity. In our day, people are more aware than ever of how difficult it is to hide our true feelings. We are sensitive to 'body language' and all that non-verbal signals can reveal.

Folly has been ruthlessly exposed and dissected. The long central section of Ecclesiastes has rubbed our noses in reality of all kinds, and we are ready now to travel with *Qoheleth* on the last stage of the journey.

PRAYER

Lord God as we live in this difficult and perplexing world, give us wisdom to hear your voice and follow in your ways. Amen.

TAKING RISKS

Mr Preacher is nearing the home straight, and these final chapters are to move us into a different atmosphere. It is worth pausing for a moment to get our bearings. In chapters 1—3 he outlined his basic thesis of the futility of life 'under the sun', while giving some hints of a world beyond that. Then in chapters 4—10 he relentlessly analysed every aspect of life, public and private, presenting an eloquent mix of comment, story, parable and observation that forced us again and again to face up to reality. Now, in a proverbial passage, he is preparing the way to approach his final assessment.

Take opportunities

The essence of life is faith, and it is to the risks of faith that *Qoheleth* now calls us. 'Casting bread upon the waters' (v. 1) probably refers to commercial voyages. 'Bread' is used in the sense of livelihood and essential goods, and it takes commitment and faith to send it out in hope of a return. But the verse has a wider application than commerce, and is advocating an attitude to life that is willing to take risks. This is amplified in the vignette in verse 2, which probably deals with being widespread in investments. 'Seven' and 'eight' suggest large measures and generosity rather than being precise numbers. The possibility of disaster is an incentive to be bold rather than an excuse to be timid. This is yet another indication that what happens in the visible world is not the full picture.

Dealing with the unknown

Much of life, as *Qoheleth* has often reminded us, is uncertain, and this uncertainty is the subject of the next few verses. Rain will pour, winds will blow, trees will fall, and it is pointless to sit around wasting away our lives. While the background to these verses is rural, they are of very wide application. Furthermore, there is mystery in our origins, and while we may know more about birth in the sense of its processes than was known when Ecclesiastes was written, the mystery of life remains as elusive as the wind (v. 5). God's works are not an open book to us, and we shall never know the answer to all life's conundrums 'under the sun'.

The response to this lack of knowledge must not be inertia, however, but rather a bold and vigorous grasping of our opportunities. We must 'sow' (v. 6)—which can, of course, refer to literal sowing, but reaches beyond that to a full engagement with life. 'Morning' and 'evening' suggest the complete day, and the idea is that each day is to be lived to the full.

Of course, Qoheleth has said many of these things before, but it is worth noting three differences in his emphasis here. The first is that these words are not mere observation but fairly sustained exhortation. There has been exhortation before, but this is more pointed. Qoheleth's final call is going to be to commitment and action. He does not want us to be paralysed by the inevitable or the unpredictable, but to live life courageously and vigorously.

The second difference is the upbeat and optimistic nature of this section. It is not about living in a fool's paradise: Qoheleth is the last person we could accuse of that. Rather, there is the sense of the over-arching providence of the creator, which is to become explicit in chapter 12.

Thirdly, this section fits well into the whole flow of the biblical revelation about life and death. Living life to the full under the threat of death is the normal biblical emphasis. Psalm 90 tells us to live in the light of death as a means of gaining wisdom; Romans 8 tells us that the love of Christ is stronger in face of death. Death is certain, but that need not make us morbid and unable to live fully and usefully. This section of Ecclesiastes tells us about the basic uncertainty of human life, yet also of its endless possibilities.

PRAYER

Lord, give us the courage to step out in faith, take risks and live our lives trusting that in everything you are working for good.
Amen.

Living Joyfully

The ominous word 'meaningless' occurs twice in this passage, but overall the impression is of life as something to be celebrated. *Qoheleth* is recommending the pursuit of happiness. This is only truly possible when the implications of futility have been faced, and is a further reminder that meaninglessness is not the last word to be spoken.

The sun is shining

As so often, we are reminded of the creation story, where the first words of God brought light into being. 'Seeing the sun' (v. 7) is more than simply existing; it is rejoicing in the goodness of God symbolized by the sunlight. The fact that there is darkness and meaninglessness does not set aside the joys of sunshine and living. It is 'sweet'—that is, to be savoured with great enjoyment. 'Days of darkness' (v. 8) are indeed part of the experience of living, but they do not ultimately cancel out the experience of joy.

Youth is for living

In verse 9, *Qoheleth* is not simply saying that the young are to be happy but that they are to pursue happiness. This involves both the mainspring of life—'the heart'—and involvement with the world around—'whatever your eyes see'. This joy is not something superficial but is a deep wellspring that directs the whole of life. The word 'follow' (more literally 'walk') refers to the outward way of life controlled by the heart. All aspects of life, outward and inward, are to be governed by joy. The eyes are the windows of the heart and they interpret what is seen. The pursuit of happiness, if it involves a genuine engagement with the world and with others, will not lapse into mere selfishness.

Moreover, joy is governed by the reality of God's judgment. 'Judgment' here has overtones of justice and moral rightness. This is no arbitrary decision. God is not like blind fate; rather, he is one who works continually to bring about his good purposes.

A salutary warning

Joy is not automatic. Youth and vigour, in themselves, are not the ends for which we were created; in fact they are meaningless (v. 10). There are problems of both heart and body that prevent us from living the life of joy. 'Anxiety' is a word that *Qoheleth* has used several times before (translated as 'grief' or 'sorrow' in 1:18; 2:23; 7:3) and it refers to vexation, grief and irritation. Indeed, 'anxiety' is the negative counterpart of 'joy', and likewise refers to the inner life. 'The troubles of the body' is a very general term, reminding us that grinding asceticism is not advocated by the Bible. Discipline is good, but not a kind of masochistic ill-treatment of our bodies.

This chapter is an encouragement not to unbridled hedonism but to a deep joy lived in the fear of God. A number of realities are prominent here. The first is the goodness of creation, the major emphasis of Genesis 1 and 2. This goodness is a reflection of God's own goodness and is still true in the fallen creation.

The second is the reality of death, something that underlies the whole book. All human aspirations and activities are overshadowed by this reality, yet in these verses that reality is a stronger incentive to live the life of joy, not a reason for despair.

The most fundamental reality of all, though, is the goodness of God. *Qoheleth* is about to present his final evidence and he has skilfully sketched two perspectives on life. For most of the book we have explored the perspective that we encounter daily, which he calls 'under the sun', and which ultimately leads to despair. Nevertheless, there is another perspective that challenges it and makes worthwhile the pursuit of joy.

REFLECTION

Are we in danger of forgetting the Bible's emphasis on joy
and allowing ourselves to see troubles and hardships
as ends in themselves?

REMEMBER YOUR CREATOR

With powerful and vivid language, *Qoheleth* sums up his message in a poem of haunting beauty. There are many obscurities in the text, although the overall meaning is fairly plain. Mr Preacher faces us with the overwhelming fact of death and urges a true response to it.

Wise words

'Remember' here (v. 1) is used with its full biblical weight. This is no perfunctory calling to mind but a resolve to commit life into the hands of the creator. The word 'creator' is a noun form of the verb 'to create' (*ba'ra*), only ever used of God in the Old Testament, and is a further echo of Genesis 1. This remembering is something to do in the glad enthusiasm of youth, not in the resigned acceptance of old age. There is also the suggestion that joylessness in old age is directly related to neglecting a relationship with God in one's youth.

Darkening world and decaying house

The language in verse 2 is vivid and compares death to the undoing of creation itself; there is a similar, longer passage in Job 3. The lights go out and a chill reigns over all. The metaphors that follow are not altogether easy to understand, but the general scene is of a great but decaying house. It may be that the details are allegorical, with 'keepers' referring to the arms, 'strong men' to the legs (see Psalm 147:10), 'grinders' to the teeth and 'those looking through the windows' to the eyes. However, translating these difficult words slightly differently, 'strong men' could mean those of high social status; 'keepers of the house', the male servants; 'grinders', female servants who make bread; and 'those who look through the windows', women of higher social status who have leisure. Together, they would represent the whole human community and its helplessness in face of death. This would probably make for a better understanding of verse 3, particularly since verses 4–5 go on to speak of human reactions to old age. Verse 4 speaks of withdrawal into the house, as life outside becomes increasingly terrifying. The second part of the verse is puzzling and may refer to restless wakefulness during the night and increasing deafness as sounds grow faint.

Verse 5 sums up the sense of decay in a number of pictures of the approach of death. There is fear of heights, and familiar streets become full of perils. The next three pictures are once again understood differently in various translations. The underlying idea appears to be the fading of desire and the swift blighting of promise. The almond tree may blossom briefly, but only to be devoured by the locusts (probably a better translation than 'grasshopper'). 'Desire' is literally 'caper plant', said to stimulate sexual desire. The whole emphasis is on a blighted landscape. The poem is powerful: the sky grows dark, the house decays and the landscape is barren.

Another house awaits, an eternal one. The journey is over and the living are left to mourn.

Dissolution of beauty

In the face of decay and death, Qoheleth repeats his warning to 'remember' (v. 6). Human life is precious and beautiful, and this is embodied in more striking imagery. The 'silver cord' and 'golden bowl' belong together in life, but death shatters them and they cannot be repaired. A pitcher is lowered into a well (probably symbolizing life and fruitfulness) by a rope around a wheel, but the whole apparatus breaks and is destroyed. The wheel probably also represents the circularity of human life. The end result (v. 7) is a return to dust and a reminder of the curse of Genesis 3:19. However, the fact that the spirit returns to God hints at a continuing life, which does not come to an end when the body decays.

A final warning

For the last time, Mr Preacher returns to his text (v. 8). He has ransacked life 'under the sun' and faced us with the last enemy, death itself. In face of that, such life is hebel, the word usually translated 'futility' or 'meaningless'. Life's value and richness and the joy that is part of it have also been underlined, however, and this causes us to look for another nuance of meaning in hebel. One such shade of meaning is 'fleeting' or 'temporary', and that would make good sense here. 'Under the sun' is not the last word; there is more to come.

PRAYER

Lord, give us wise and open hearts to face the changes of life and the reality of death, trusting in you who made us and have good purposes for us. Amen.

The ONE SHEPHERD

The book closes with an epilogue bringing out more clearly the underlying message of Mr Preacher. Some commentators have argued that this is a 'orthodox' attempt to reconcile *Qoheleth*'s scepticism with the rest of the Old Testament message. However, this ignores the way in which he has frequently implied that there is another world beyond the futility of life under the sun; the epilogue now makes it explicit. The epilogue falls into two parts: the first in verses 9–12 and the second in verses 13–14, which we shall study in the next reading.

Scholar and teacher

Qoheleth exemplifies the best kind of teacher. He is wise (v. 9)—and we have noted the many and varied ways in which this word suggests not only knowledge but character. He saw that he was given wisdom, not as his personal possession but as something to share with others. Moreover, he did his research and what he presented was cogent and orderly. The words used suggest his diligence. He 'pondered': that is, he weighed the evidence and chose his words with care. 'Searched out' suggests thoroughness and diligence. 'Set in order' shows skill and aesthetic sensitivity in presentation. His chosen medium was 'proverbs', a word that includes parables, riddles, allegory, story and other rhetorical devices.

Here is a fine picture of the good preacher or teacher, and it should be considered carefully by all who try to preach, teach and write. There is no substitute for the hard work, research and imaginative engagement exemplified here. As verse 10 asserts, the author is writing truth, not merely his opinions. That truth is expressed in 'just the right words'—more literally, 'words of delight', which appeal and give pleasure. They are also 'upright' words, which implies orderliness. Truth is beautiful and also organized!

General application

What applies to the words of *Qoheleth* applies to all the wise (v. 11). Here the emphasis is on the effectiveness of their kind of teaching. Having emphasized the beauty and clarity of wise words, we now know how pain as well as pleasure is at the heart of learning. Two images are used. 'Goads'—used to prod an animal into action— suggests that the aim of teaching is to stimulate us to action. 'Nails' suggests that the teaching is firmly fixed in the mind. 'Collected sayings' well describes the book of Ecclesiastes and, for that matter, Proverbs, and underlines the importance of written as well as oral teaching.

All this, vital as it is, might give the impression that being a teacher involves no more than human diligence, research, industry, imagination and an organized mind. These are certainly needed, but one vital ingredient remains. The teaching is 'given by one Shepherd' (v. 11). The Shepherd is God (see Psalms 23 and 80), and thus the finished product, while clearly the words of humans, is also the word of God. The human contribution, as we have seen, is indispensable, but remains lifeless unless God is in it. Remembering the creator is linked very specifically with listening to and acting in accordance with his words.

No additions

Revelation 22:18–19 warns against adding to or subtracting from the words already given. A similar warning is given here (v. 12). That does not mean that *Qoheleth* has said everything there is to say, but that there is a wisdom which is false and dangerous, and we must be on our guard against it. Not all that is written is of value: 'Of making many books there is no end.' In these days of computers, websites and other such aids to fast production, this is even more true than in the author's time. But it is doubtful if that is all the author is saying. It is, after all, a trite statement and 'many' implies 'no end'. In fact, what he is saying follows on from the first part of the verse, that many books have no useful end; they contribute nothing. It is in this context that 'much study' is to be seen. After all, *Qoheleth* has just emphasized that study and diligence are at the heart of good teaching. There is also a realistic sense of human frailty and a wholesome regard for human weariness.

REFLECTION

Those who teach need to saturate all their work with prayer, and those who listen and read need to pray for their teachers.

The CONCLUSION *of the* MATTER

Like 'firmly embedded nails' the message is now hammered home and we turn from form to substance.

This book has not been a collection of random comments, as some have argued. A definite journey has been travelled and the goal has been reached. So far, there have been hints of a world where all is not *hebel*; now Mr Preacher is to be explicit. Here he is illustrating the point he has made in the previous verses: the book will not be pointless.

What is it to be human?

The NIV reads, 'this is the whole duty of every human being' (v. 13), but there is no word for 'duty' in the Hebrew text. What is being said here is not that there is an obligation for humans, but that this is what being human is about. Only in this way can we be truly what we were created to be. So, what is the 'whole' of being human? First of all, it is to fear God. This will free us from the crippling fears with which this book abounds: fear of oppression, poverty, exploitation, old age and death. The fear of God is reverence for his greatness and holiness, which leads to a life of dependence, worship and integrity. That will enable us to see a far horizon and avoid being trapped 'under the sun'.

Second, it is to keep his commandments. Verse 13 is the only time in the book that God's commandments have been mentioned. This is an important reminder that the fear of God is not simply a feeling. The emotions are important, but they must lead to transformed conduct. It is also linked to the fact that God is the creator. Since he has made us for himself, we cannot become what he intended us to be unless he is at the centre of our lives.

What will the end be?

Earlier, *Qoheleth* spoke of judgment (3:17; 11:9), and here he shows that nothing will be hidden from God's verdict. At first sight, this statement may seem terrifying. It is indeed terrifying, but there is more to it than that. The whole burden of the book has been the mystery of life and death, and the sense of meaninglessness that comes from our inability to know what will succeed and what will not. The affirmation is made that everything has significance. Good will be rewarded and evil punished. Not until the death and resurrection of Jesus will we see how this will happen, but here we are being called to the life of faith, a genuine realism.

Our journey with *Qoheleth* has taken us into many strange places and caused us to face many hard questions. Let us now consider four concluding issues. First, *Qoheleth* emphasizes the questions that arise in the life of faith. He compels us to wrestle with such questions and that we will not reach maturity unless we do so. Time and again he has dismissed facile solutions and has forced us to face up to reality.

Second, he gives human wisdom and achievement a fair run for their money. He is not a cynic who simply dismisses and condemns without giving a fair hearing. Creation, history, power, culture, beauty and pleasure are all shown to be wanting if seen as ends in themselves. If seen as gifts and received gratefully, though, they can be appreciated and enjoyed.

Third, *Qoheleth* draws very heavily on the theology of the opening chapters of Genesis. Creation and Fall are woven into the texture of the book and, as we have often noted in this commentary, it is against the broader biblical backdrop that Ecclesiastes must be seen.

Fourth, the book impels us beyond itself. The huge questions it raises can only be answered in the light of the New Testament. For example, in Romans 8:20–25, Paul talks of the creation being subject to futility but of God's plans to remove that futility and bring about a new heaven and a new earth. The wonder of the new creation can only be fully realized when we have faced the discords and brokenness of the fallen creation, and this is what *Qoheleth* has made us do. Yet he has also given us glimpses of the world beyond, and, by pointing us to the eternity that God has placed in our hearts, has given us an outlook that helps us to navigate the perils of this life.

REFLECTION

*Paul also uses the word meaning 'futile' or 'in vain' in
1 Corinthians. As we leave Ecclesiastes, we do so with this as our
concluding reflection:*

*'Therefore, my dear brothers and sisters, stand firm. Let nothing
move you. Always give yourselves fully to the work of the Lord,
because you know that your labour in the Lord is not in vain.'*

1 Corinthians 15:58

WHAT IS IT ABOUT?

'All the ages are not worth the day in which the Song of Songs was given to Israel; for all the writings are holy, but the Song of Songs is the Holy of Holies' (Rabbi Aqiba, died AD135). This is one of the earliest but by no means the last of the fulsome compliments heaped on this short book. There are few books, however, whose meaning has been disputed so fiercely and whose interpretations have been so bewilderingly diverse.

The basic premise of this commentary is that the Song is a celebration of the joys of love springing from the creation of humanity in the image of God. We shall see how the early chapters of Genesis are frequently drawn on by the author.

The title

Verse 1 is in effect the title of the book. The Hebrew construction 'Song of Songs', used in most modern translations of the Bible, consists of the same noun given in the singular and plural, and is a common way of expressing the superlative. We can compare it with such phrases as 'king of kings', 'holy of holies' and 'heaven of heavens'. It suggests the greatest and most sublime of songs.

Was it written by Solomon? If so, that places it in the mid-tenth century BC. It is virtually impossible to date the song in terms of its language, which shows many peculiarities and includes many words found nowhere else in the Bible, or only very rarely. Certainly Solomon is associated with an outburst of literary activity (1 Kings 4:32). Moreover, he is remembered as an insatiable lover (1 Kings 11:3).

The Hebrew preposition *le* could mean not only 'by', which implies Solomonic authorship, but could also mean 'to'—that is, dedicated to Solomon. Or it could mean 'relating to'—that is, 'in the Solomonic wisdom tradition'. Undoubtedly the Solomon connection is of some importance in interpreting what follows, but this cannot be discussed without looking another question: who are the characters in the poem?

The characters

It is reasonably certain that there is one main female character, in some versions called 'the beloved', a country girl who speaks most of the lines in the poem. The main problem centres around the identity of the male character or characters. Some argue for a fairly elaborate plot: the girl falls in love with a young shepherd boy; then she is seen by Solomon, who snatches her away to his harem, from which she eventually escapes.

The view taken here, however, is that there are two main characters: the girl ('the beloved') and the man ('the lover'). There is also an undefined group called the 'friends' or 'daughters of Jerusalem', who act as a kind of chorus. The significance of Solomon will be discussed in the relevant passages.

The interpretation

This is a poem with a riot of colour and imagery whose main theme is the celebration of human sexuality in the mutual relationship of a woman and a man. But is there more? What about the view that the book is an allegory of Yahweh's love for Israel and Christ's love for the Church? Allegorical interpretations rest on a simple basic assumption: that the text is about something other than it appears to be, that every word, image, character and action corresponds to some spiritual reality. To put it another way, the song is ostensibly about human love but in reality is about God's love.

I want to argue that the song is about both divine and human love. Human love reflects God's love in the way that the moon reflects the sun. Human love is a tributary of the great river of God's love. Holding these two kinds of love in tension, we can see different levels of meaning throughout the song. It is a love story of a real man and a real woman and it is also the story of God the great lover, of which the human stories are mere sub-plots. This commentary will attempt to do justice to both levels.

The story

Not all commentators agree that the song is a unified poem, much less that a coherent story underlies it. My basic assumption, however, is that there is a simple storyline, beginning with a springtime romance (chs.1 and 2), progressing to a wedding and honeymoon (chs. 3 and 4), and going on to problems after marriage and then a kind of second honeymoon (chs. 5—8).

REFLECTION

Love is not so much a part of our lives
as the context in which we live.

KISSING & TELLING

The words 'kiss and tell' encapsulate what it is to fall in love: the intense intimacy and fascination, and the impossibility of keeping it to ourselves. These verses do much to create the atmosphere and ambience of the song, as it begins with a relationship already dawning. The words (apart from a brief intervention by the friends in verse 4) are a passionate declaration of the woman's love.

Love's passion

The woman takes the initiative in verse 2. This young woman has seen a handsome young shepherd and fallen in love with him; her heart beats, her throat is dry and the whole world is transformed. The whole experience is physical, full-blooded and passionate. She longs for his kisses, and she expresses this longing in the metaphor of wine with its rich bouquet as well as its taste. This merges into the imagery of perfume, which adds the sense of smell to that of taste and powerfully suggests the heady atmosphere of love.

This perfume is particularly associated, in the woman's mind, with the lover's name (v. 3), which is nowhere revealed in the song. There is profound significance in names in the biblical world. Names are not just convenient handles; they convey the essence of the person. Is it not the case that when someone falls in love, the name of the loved one, until then ordinary and insignificant, bursts into life?

What are the other associations of 'name'? At the very heart of the faith of the Old Testament is the sacred name of Israel's God: for example, 'O Lord, our Lord, how majestic is your name in all the earth' (Psalm 8:1) and 'Praise the Lord, O my soul; all my inmost being, praise his holy name' (Psalm 103:1). In the New Testament, perhaps the most striking example is, 'Therefore God exalted him to the highest place and gave him the name that is above every name, that at the name of Jesus every knee should bow' (Philippians 2:9–10).

The kissing is the foretaste of greater intimacy: 'take me away with you' (v. 4). The NRSV's 'draw me' is a better translation, with its idea of mysterious attraction. Significantly, this word is used by the prophets about the love of Yahweh, which draws his people to him:

'I have loved you with an everlasting love; I have drawn you with loving-kindness' (Jeremiah 31:3); and 'I led them with cords of human kindness, with ties of love' (Hosea 11:4).

Those who see three main characters in the song interpret verse 4 as the girl's plea to her lover to save her from the clutches of Solomon, who has already taken her into his chambers. It is far more likely, however, that the young shepherd has already become a king in her eyes, and her mind is racing ahead to a time of more intimate union and exclusive love, away from prying eyes and critical voices.

Verse 4b is the first intervention of the friends and suggests that her love has inspired them all.

Love's defence

The girl fears that she will not be attractive to the one she loves: 'Dark I am, yet lovely' (v. 5). Her dark skin would be an indicator of lower class: she works in the field and is therefore sunburnt (v. 6), in contrast to the paler girls in the more sophisticated setting of Jerusalem.

This sense of inadequacy is compounded by the mention of her brothers' anger and their insistence that she care for the vineyards (this may help to explain the odd verses 8:8–9 discussed later). On one level this may merely suggest that they made her work in the hot sun, but the imagery in the song is multi-layered and probably the vineyard refers to the girl herself and her own burgeoning sexuality.

In a manner that the reader soon recognizes to be typical of the song, the image of the vineyard merges into that of keeping sheep (v. 7) and the girl addresses her lover. She wants to be alone with him, away from the lecherous looks and ribald talk of the other shepherds. The reference to veiled women could suggest mourning (see, for example, 2 Samuel 15:30), but the whole atmosphere is more reminiscent of Genesis 38:14–15, where Tamar's veil is taken by Judah as the normal sign of a prostitute. This woman's love is faithful and exclusive.

PRAYER

Lord, give us hearts to love and wills to be faithful so that our love on earth may reflect that in heaven. Amen.

MUTUAL LOVE

The story now develops with entire naturalness and yet consummate artistry as love begins to grow. I think it is more likely that verse 8 belongs to the man than to the friends (as in NIV), since she has just addressed a question to him (1:7). He is by no means blind to her attractions: 'most beautiful of women'. His first endearment, 'my darling' (v. 9), is followed by the assertion that putting a girl like her in a crowd of shepherds is like setting a mare loose among the stallions who pull Pharaoh's chariots. He praises her good taste in jewellery and promises her more.

She replies (vv. 12–14) that he is a king to her and she wants to be in his arms. Her language, characteristically for the Song, is sensual and evokes the beauties both of the human body and of nature. Here the heady perfumes of the royal banquet and the leafy oasis of En-Gedi on the western shore of the Dead Sea are evoked. En-Gedi, although surrounded by a desolate landscape, is a particularly beautiful oasis with a waterfall and stream. Its remoteness is part of its attraction.

This merges into a teasing and bantering exchange (1:15—2:2) that captures beautifully their growing passion for each other. He dwells on her eyes, those windows into her heart, and both are anticipating the consummation of their love: 'our bed is verdant' (v. 16). The word usually translated 'bed' has implications of elaborate carving, and, since this appears to be an outdoor scene, may refer to the leafy branches in the garden. Similarly, the word for 'house' (v. 17) is plural and may mean the trees of the garden.

Modestly, the woman disparages her own attractiveness: 'I am a rose of Sharon' (v. 1). Sharon is a plain between the coast and the hills north of Jaffa, not noted for any natural beauty. The lily of the valleys was as common and as nondescript a plant as you could see. But the man robustly defends her: 'This lily stands out among the brambles.'

Mirroring God's love

We should notice the unselfishness that is at the heart of genuine love. These two have eyes only for each other and their mutual praise is eloquent and sincere. In such love we find an answer to the selfishness at the heart of human sinfulness. We can glimpse how it is that such love mirrors that of God himself and provides the anticipation of heaven. Love is at root unselfish and thus mirrors God's own love, which loves us as we are.

We should also note how each sees the other transformed. He is a king and she is a lily among the thorns. This again is close to the heart of the gospel, where Christ transforms sinful people into likenesses of himself.

The Bible speaks of love in many ways. Sometimes, as in 1 Corinthians 13, love is analysed as a antidote to triumphalism and arrogance. Sometimes, as in the book of Ruth, love is the subject of a story, and its mysterious workings are shown played out in ordinary lives. Sometimes, as here in the Song, it is realized in lyrical imagery. No comment is made, but our hearts and imaginations are powerfully stirred. All of these methods of communication are employed in the Bible's characteristic appeals to mind, heart and will. The purpose of poetry is not to teach us doctrine but to show us what love is like.

REFLECTION

This love is youthful but need not be confined to the young. The grace of God can renew our hearts with this kind of love, even when many years have passed.

A SPRINGTIME ROMANCE

Now the girl takes up the song as they playfully romp through the forest. Her lover is a magnificent figure and stands out because of his ripeness and virility: 'like an apple tree among the trees of the forest' (v. 3). The idea of celebration continues in verse 4: 'He has taken me to the banquet hall.' This, like the 'bed' and the 'house', may be the vineyard itself. Then, drained with their mutual passion, they lie in each other's arms.

In verses 8 and 9 the lover himself arrives, his ardour evoked by a series of vigorous verbs: 'leaping', 'bounding', and then 'gazing' and 'peering'. It is spring, the whole world is exploding into life and fragrance, and he calls her to join in. Who can deny that it was a most successful first date?

Their love is mutual

In this passage, there is a celebration of physical passion and a frankness and lack of sentimentality that avoid both smuttiness and prudery. The romantic associations of wine, flowers, forests and fruit are exploited and their resonances are full of power.

What are we to make of this? We shall begin by considering verse 7: 'Daughters of Jerusalem, I charge you by the gazelles and by the does of the field: Do not arouse or awaken love until it so desires.' This expression occurs again in 3:5, and a similar expression can be found in 8:4. Gazelles and does occur in Sumerian and Canaanite love poetry as symbols of sexual potency. The verse appears to be an appeal for spontaneity in love, an appeal not to force it but to let it develop and blossom. This kind of love is too special simply to be thrown around; this love is for each other alone. We have seen how the song can be read as a celebration of humanity in the image of God. Genesis 2:24 speaks of a man and woman becoming 'one flesh' in a new and organic relationship, which cannot be shared with anyone else.

True love is always a developing and growing experience. Here we have a progression from sitting to eating (v. 3), to the inner room (v. 4), to the fond embrace (v. 6). Thus the private and subjective experience of love is expressed in a series of vivid and haunting images which are yet evocative of universal experience.

Underneath these developing images are deeper levels, which we can discern when we consider the wider biblical context of the song. The word 'shade' in verse 3 is used many times in terms of divine protection—for example, in Psalm 121:5, 'The Lord is your shade at your right hand'; and in Hosea 14:7, 'People will dwell under his shade', in the context of protection against Assyria. True love, whether human or divine, is robust and bracing. The phrase 'his banner over me is love' (v. 4) suggests an ensign and protection against marauders. 'His left arm is under my head' (v. 6) reminds us that 'arm' is a regular Old Testament term for the protecting power of God.

Their love affects their surroundings

The lovers exult in the beauty of nature as it bursts back into life at spring. As already noted, the vivid verbs used about the lover's approach join their romance with nature's joyful awakening. Many passages in the Psalter celebrate creation in such terms (for example, Psalms 65:12–13; 98:7–8; 147:7–8).

So here in the Song, love paints the whole world in beautiful colours and the lovers' hearts beat along with the life surging through the earth. A few well-chosen phrases sharply and memorably evoke the spring, and the winter rains giving way to bloom, fragrance and song. Thus the lovers become part of the returning life of creation.

Again, this leads us to the deeper resonances of the words. The fig tree is used in Zechariah 3:10 as a symbol of the peace and prosperity of the coming kingdom: 'In that day each of you will invite his neighbour to sit under his vine and fig tree.' Jesus also speaks of the fig tree as a sign of his coming and the dawning of the new creation: 'Now learn this lesson from the fig tree: as soon as its twigs get tender and its leaves come out, you know that summer is near. Even so, when you see these things happening, you know that it is near, right at the door' (Mark 13:28–29).

One of the words used of the lover is 'leaping' (v. 8), and this also occurs in Isaiah 35:6, telling how the lame will be healed in the new creation: 'then will the lame leap like a deer'. The whole landscape is alive with the presence of the creator.

REFLECTION

In the midst of our broken world and sinful lives, we can yet catch
glimpses of the world to come that can transform the present.

BE WATCHFUL

The Song is not sentimental escapism and our author now turns for the first time to the things that threaten love's young dream. This little section can usefully be studied in two parts.

The threats

In verse 14 the man speaks directly. His beloved appears to be in a barren landscape, contrasted with the spring landscape of the vineyard and garden. Again he praises her beauty.

A particular threat from the barren landscape comes in verse 15, a text whose meaning is rather elusive. Perhaps the 'little foxes' are the other young shepherds who lay siege to the girl. The 'vineyard', in that case, would be the girl herself. This, combined with the idea in the previous verse of how difficult it is to gain access to the beloved, is an indication that, while love is natural and spontaneous, it must be cultivated and protected and not taken for granted. Some commentators point out that in some Egyptian love poetry, foxes stand for sexually aggressive men.

Whatever the specific connotations, it is plain that there is a warning here not to regard love as something that cannot be threatened. In the raptures of early love, it is all too easy to imagine that such emotion will last for ever. One of the emphases of the Song as it develops is that love will be attacked but can emerge stronger and deeper from such troubles.

The promises

In verses 16–17, we have reassurance and renewed declarations of love from the girl. First there is a statement of mutual belonging: 'My lover is mine and I am his.' The fact that this is repeated in reverse order in 6:3 shows us that here is a relationship of true equality and mutuality. This has a fascinating parallel in the words God uses of his covenant with his people: 'I will be their God and they will be my people' (Jeremiah 7:23; 11:4; Ezekiel 34:30). Once again, human love echoes divine love. This is no passing attraction but a deep commitment.

That commitment is also the theme of the beautiful expression in verse 17, 'Until the day breaks and the shadows flee'. This can be understood in two opposite ways. The first phrase reads literally 'until the day breathes'. This could refer to a light breeze in late afternoon and the lengthening shadows as evening approaches—similar to Genesis 3:8 where God walks in Eden in 'the cool of the day'. On the other hand, it could refer to the light breeze that heralds the dawn. Probably there is a deliberate ambiguity here: love is a total experience that fills time and also transcends it.

The other details in the vignette are hard to interpret. 'He browses among the lilies' (v. 16) may have sexual connotations as well as being a sign of spring. Gazelles and young stags in heat in springtime are another reminder of the physicality of love.

Chapters 1 and 2 have indeed been like the wine mentioned in 1:2, heady and sensuous and appealing to all our senses. God loves us as whole people and this Song celebrates the joy of touch, the ambience of love, the sounds and experiences of intimate relationship. It is a reminder that the topic of sexuality is one that can be discussed and taught in Christian circles. It is likewise a warning not to treat sex as an idol and to realize that there are dangers in love and sexuality.

We must also bear in mind the developing story. Some commentators have argued that there cannot be a consistent story since, for example, 8:8–10 appears to say that the couple are not married, but that can equally be understood as a reminiscence or perhaps a second honeymoon. We are now to see how this love fares in the wear and tear of life and the onslaughts of death, the subject of the following chapters.

PRAYER

Lord God, whose love gives us others to love and to love us, may our love in some way reflect your great love for us in Jesus Christ.
Amen.

WHAT DREAMS MAY COME

After the springtime romance of chapters 1 and 2, events begin to move quickly as we come to the middle section of the Song. I shall argue that in 3:6–11 we have the actual wedding of the two lovers, but before that we have this tense little section, which carries on the theme of the threats to love at the end of the previous chapter.

The dream

Not all commentators see these verses as a dream sequence, but I want to suggest some indications which point in that direction. The first is the rather shadowy nature of the section (contrast this with the vivid imagery of the wedding in 3:6–11), places merging into each other as they do in dreams. Many people will have experienced that particular eerie nightmare in which you are in a place, apparently familiar, possibly to meet someone well known, but however hard you try or far you walk you find yourself endlessly wandering into more and more unknown territory. Such is the girl's ordeal here, and all who have known that kind of dream will sympathize with her. The threats to love come not only from outside but from inner fears and imagination.

The city

Here (and in the parallel passage in 5:2–7) the city is a hostile place and contrasts with the safety of the bedroom and garden. Indeed it is another version of the 'desert' that we shall study in the next section. There is irony in that while the girl is searching for her lover, she herself is found by the watchmen (v. 3), whose shadowiness contributes to the general eery feeling of the place.

The city is to appear in a positive light in 6:4, however, and this reminds us of the flexibility and richness of metaphor in the Song.

The meeting

In the manner of dreams, the search is followed immediately by the unexpected appearance of the lover, who is consequently brought to the maternal home. The mention of the mother's house at this point is significant. We are moving close to a wedding, given the role that mothers had in arranging marriages for their daughters. In Genesis 24:67, Isaac and Rebekah consummate their marriage in Isaac's mother's tent. Similarly, Naomi urges her two widowed daughters-in-law to return to their mothers' houses (Ruth 1:8).

Once again, in verse 5, the charge first seen in 2:7 occurs. We saw there how gazelles and does are associated with sexual potency. Love must take its natural course. The Hebrew uses what is often called an 'oath formula', although such expressions usually include the divine name, for example, 'Lord of hosts'. This underlines the seriousness and magnitude of love which, on a the eve of a wedding, is most appropriate.

This short section has a number of functions in the development of the Song. It is a reminder that the story is set in the real world, not simply an idealized pastoral 'neverland'. It further shows that love needs to be disciplined and await its natural development. The rest of the Bible celebrates marriage (in Genesis 2:22–24, God, as father of the bride, brings Eve to Adam; and this act is echoed in Ephesians 5:31–32), so we would expect the Song to celebrate it too. This section is an important preparation for the wedding that is to follow.

REFLECTION

Love in a world like ours cannot remain immune from fears and worries. It is vital, at such times, to trust in God and be faithful.

COMING UP *from the* DESERT

Twice in the Song, in 3:6 and 8:5, occurs the phrase 'coming up from the desert'. Commentators have made little of it, but I want to suggest that it is crucial to the interpretation of the song. In this section we shall examine two issues: the desert itself and the significance of Solomon.

The desert

The desert is one of the great biblical motifs. The Song of Songs came to be associated with the Passover, which cannot be separated in our thinking from the desert wanderings of the Israelites. I am not suggesting that the Song is an allegory of the exodus event. Rather, the inner significance of that event, the great romance of Yahweh with his people, is being repeated in this love story of a girl and a boy. The desert is associated with guidance in cloud and fire—'like a column of smoke' (v. 6; Exodus 13:21)—and with a portable shrine, like the tent in the desert (v. 7).

Even earlier than the exodus, biblical story records the desert wanderings of Abraham and Sarah, ancestors of their race (Genesis 20:1). This 'desert' is not so much a sandy waste like the Sahara, but a stony barren land known as the Negev, that arid region where the Judean highlands merge into the rocky wasteland around the Dead Sea. We need to read the Song in canonical context, aware of the depth added by seeing it as part of the great story of God's involvement in human affairs.

Moreover, the image of the desert, as already noted, relates to the previous section, in which the mean streets of the city are another version of the desert. Just as the love of the boy and the girl had been linked with the landscape transformed by spring, so the absence of the lover is reflected in wilderness surroundings.

The 'desert' has always been a vital place in the growth of understanding and love for God. Moses, Paul, and many others withdrew into the desert to learn more deeply of God, and returned to the business of life refreshed and renewed. Love is a great stripping away of illusions and the opening of the eyes to reality. In the desert, all the normal props and securities with which we surround ourselves are stripped away. Yet the desert is never an end in itself, and we are now ready for the 'coming up' (v. 6).

Solomon

In verse 7 we have the first mention of Solomon since chapter 1, and how we interpret this is crucial in the unfolding interpretation of the Song. Those who argue that Solomon is a character in the story use this passage as part of the evidence. It is much more likely, however, given the earlier use of royal imagery, that in her excitement the girl is comparing her young man to Solomon and seeing her wedding as if it were a royal occasion. Some ancient Jewish commentators allude to the practice of brides and bridegrooms wearing crowns on their wedding day.

Once again the opulence of the Solomonic entourage is emphasized. A passage that gives a useful comparison is Psalm 45. For example, see verse 8: 'All your robes are fragrant with myrrh and aloes and cassia; from palaces adorned with ivory the music of the strings makes you glad.' This psalm is usually taken to refer to a royal wedding, although some have argued that it is in fact an ordinary bride and bridegroom who feel like, and are treated as, royalty on their wedding day.

Bearing in mind the biblical idea that marriage is a picture of Christ's love for the church (Ephesians 5:32), it is perhaps significant that in verse 11 the 'friends' or 'daughters of Jerusalem' are called 'daughters of Zion'. Zion, the city, who is also the bride, appears again in Revelation 21:2 as the Lamb's wife.

So here we have the marriage, and the two become one flesh. The time for greater and fuller intimacy has arrived. But before we leave this section, in case we imagine we are moving into a world of unrealistic sentimentality, there is a sober awareness of the dangers that love has to face. Solomon's warriors are armed and 'prepared for the terrors of the night' (v. 8). This phrase in Psalm 91:5 suggests supernatural enemies, and, if that is the shade of the meaning here, it would anticipate the 'waters' and 'rivers' of 8:7, for which I shall suggest a supernatural interpretation.

PRAYER

Lord, we thank you for your gift of love and relationships. We ask that your will may be at their centre and touch them with your love, through Jesus Christ our Lord. Amen.

HOW BEAUTIFUL YOU ARE

The bridegroom now praises his new bride in language that complements the external opulence of the wedding. This type of poem, of which there are a number in the Song, is often described as being similar to the Arabic *wasf*. '*Wasf*' is an Arabic term meaning fundamentally 'description'. Songs used at Syrian weddings in the 19th century by the groom and the bride elaborated on each other's physical attractions. In contrast to the publicity of the wedding, this is an intimate and exclusive poem.

The imagery

Tastes vary from culture to culture. It is highly unlikely that any girl today would be flattered by comparisons with mountain goats (v. 1) and sheep emerging from a dip (v. 2), still less with military fortification (v. 4). Love talk is personal, and sounds strange and embarrassing if overheard.

It is worth examining one of these images a little more closely to find a clue as to how they work: 'Your neck is like the tower of David, built with elegance; on it hang a thousand shields, all of them shields of warriors' (v. 4). Taken as a simple comparison, this is absurd, and plainly there is no suggestion of visual correspondence. In fact, it is probably an image suggesting power and dignity, with the further nuance of elegance. The name 'David' adds depth and is one of the many links of the Song with wider biblical context. The shields, prosaically, may refer to necklaces, but also suggest the idea of protection.

The theology

It may seem odd to use the word 'theology' to describe such a frankly erotic poem, but that is to miss the point. Just as chapter 2 has rejoiced in the beauty of God's creation, so here the poet rejoices in the beauty of the human body. This is part of what it is to believe that humanity is in the image of God. We have to hold this reality together with the other reality of sinfulness and fallenness.

In connection with the Song's frank delight in the beauty of the human body, there is an illuminating passage in 1 Corinthians 6:13: 'The body is not meant for sexual immorality...'. What is fascinating is that Paul does not go on to say some such phrase as 'but for morality', 'but for purity' or the like. What he does say is 'but for the Lord'. This immediately raises the whole thing to a different dimension: this kind of love is neither plunging through a bog of steamy sensuality nor grimly walking a tightrope of legalism, but celebrating the love that became incarnate in Jesus.

This is why I believe that the early instincts of both Jewish and Christian commentators on the Song, in spite of allegorical extravagances, were profoundly right to see in the love of a man and a woman a reflection of the love of God. It is this that lies at the heart of the great biblical word 'covenant', which is not a contract between solicitors but a marriage relationship.

Here the woman, in the context of a loving marriage, is praised for her beauty. Thus, the man recognizes that she is not merely his possession; she is to be affirmed as a person in her own right. This is the kind of affirmation possible only in the context of a stable and exclusive relationship.

Good relationships

Many people today are emotionally damaged. This is often because of a lack of affirmation in childhood or, worse, because of abuse, sometimes physical, sometimes verbal. The British 'stiff upper lip' and difficulty in expressing emotions were often praised in the past as the right way to behave. The kind of love expressed so vividly here calls us to self-giving and to romance as an ongoing feature of our relationships. God loves us with the tenderness and passion of a parent for a child (see Psalm 103:13). This gives to worship a sense of intimacy as well as wonder, and of joy as well as reverence.

This marriage is not about rules but about relationship, hence the delight and freshness of the imagery. Once again, the permanence of their love is emphasized in the phrase already discussed in chapter 2: 'Until the day breaks and the shadows flee'. This love is for the whole person; it is permanent and, as such, echoes God's own love.

REFLECTION

For this reason a man will leave his father and mother and be united to his wife, and the two will become one flesh. This is a profound mystery—but I am talking about Christ and the church.

Ephesians 5:31–32

The HONEYMOON

The use of the word 'bride', which appears in the Song only in this section, is a further hint that the wedding has just taken place. Its repetition confirms the freshness and newness of the experience, and as the poem develops we move into further realms of imagery.

The invitation

We are not to imagine, from verse 8, that the woman is literally roaming the northern mountains. The mountain range of Hermon, which extends into Lebanon, is in the extreme north of Israel. The point is that the lover wants all distance to be removed. Mountains are also the haunt of wild animals and he wants her away from danger.

He again compliments her and her attraction for him (v. 9). Here he uses the word 'sister' (see further comments on 8:1, p. 166), and this introduces the idea of the organic relationship of the man and woman, like that of siblings. It is important to realize that 'sister' does not convey any nuance of incest. In love poetry of the ancient Near East, 'sister' is used as a term of endearment in a marriage relationship.

The garden

Wine, milk and honey (vv. 10–11) were characteristic of the promised land after the desert wanderings of the Israelites (see, for example, Deuteronomy 6:3; 7:13; 11:9). For this couple, the desert has become a garden. In verse 12 we have the first mention of a garden in the Song, though there have been hints of it in chapter 1. The garden is described as 'locked up' and 'sealed' because until her wedding night the woman has kept herself for her lover.

There are two particular features of this garden: exuberant, fragrant growth and a bubbling spring. In one sense, verses 13–14 are unrealistic because no ancient garden would have contained such a wide range of plants. However, the emphasis is on the incomparable beauty of the beloved, so nature is being ransacked to provide examples of fragrance and loveliness. There is also, I suggest, a deeper level. Among the kaleidoscope of images, a particular recurring pattern can be discerned. We are, in effect, back in the garden of Eden, in the days of innocence when marriage was instituted and the command to procreate given. Like that garden, this one is filled with 'trees that were pleasing to the eye and good for food' (Genesis 2:9). In Eden, the tasting of forbidden fruits had disastrous consequences and led to the wasteland of thorns, thistles and barren soil with which Genesis 3 ends. Here, though, the desert has been transformed by love, which is symbolized by the tasting of fruits (v. 16). This in turn points forward to the new creation where 'the leaves of the tree are for the healing of the nations' (Revelation 22:2).

The spring of water (v. 15), with its freshness and movement, is the life-force producing growth and beauty. The wider implications are again clearer when we think of Eden: 'A river watering the garden flowed from Eden' (Genesis 2:10).

That river flows through scripture. There are many references in the Psalter, suggesting that this idea was central to Israel's praise of God. See, for example, Psalm 46:4, in which the 'holy place' must mean paradise rather than Jerusalem, which has no river. In Psalm 65:9, the river fructifies the land: 'The streams of God are filled with water to provide the people with grain'. Another clear reference is Ezekiel 47, where, in a vision of the new Jerusalem, a river flows from the temple to irrigate the barren lands around the Dead Sea. All these passages have in common the idea of life-giving water and the desert blossoming as the rose.

Two other references from the New Testament underline this idea. In John 7:38, Jesus himself identifies the river with the Holy Spirit: 'Whoever believes in me, as the Scripture has said, streams of living water will flow from within him' (John 7:38). Finally, in Revelation 22:1, 'the river of the water of life' flows from the throne of God.

The images of the tree and water are complemented by that of wind (v. 16). The winds blowing on the garden can be read as symbols of the creating Spirit as well as the powerful rush of love between the man and the woman.

The entrance of the lover into the garden in 5:1 is the moment of consummation. Here he speaks to her as a husband to a wife; the spices, honey, wine and milk all echo the earlier poem in chapter 4 and indicate the climax of the wedding. The final words of the 'friends' appear to be a celebration of the union.

PRAYER

Lord, we ask that those about to be married will find their deepest longings and hopes mirrored here. We pray too that those long married may find their love renewed and refreshed. Amen.

A Lovers' Tiff

Another dream?

The previous two sections covered the wedding and the honeymoon. However, all is not well and what we have here may be described as a 'lovers' tiff'. The man comes knocking at the woman's door, but she has undressed and washed and is deliciously comfortable in bed and cannot be bothered to get up (vv. 2–3). Then she feels her passion rising and eventually rises to open the door, only to find that he is gone (vv. 5–6). There follows another frantic dash through the streets, this time more frightening as she is mugged by the watchmen, and desperately she appeals to the 'daughters of Jerusalem' (v. 7).

An obvious question is whether this section, like 3:1–4, is a dream sequence. It could be evoking the semi-awake state of late at night or early in the morning, or possibly it begins as a semi-dream followed by a realistic account. A rather obvious parallel would be the experience of dozing early in the morning, hearing a bell in a dream, and then realizing that it is the alarm clock.

A rude awakening

Verses 4 and 5 have been seen by some to contain sexual innuendo. This is not impossible, but it does not fit easily with the man's disappearance. It may be that the dream–reality sequence of the section is a clue to its meaning. The dream part may include erotic imagery, but the realistic part probably refers to an actual account. In any case, petulance and carelessness lead to a break in the relationship, and subsequent panic and distress.

Complacency is always a real danger after the raptures of first love. After the honeymoon there is the unglamorous business of beginning the daily grind. This is dramatized in the phrase, 'I slept but my heart was awake' (v. 2). In the somnolent state it seemed that the passion of early love could continue without daily discipline and sheer hard work. This is a profound mystery, but the main way in which love is shown to be real is in consistent loving.

On the spiritual as well as the physical level, this has enormous significance. It is very easy to idle our lives away, professing love for

Jesus in dreamy choruses until he comes knocking and finds us in a lukewarm state. It is easy to keep him waiting: 'Not now; but when I've finished my degree... when I settle down in my job... when the children are older...', or another excuse. These are legitimate concerns, but it is a question of priorities. There are times when God withdraws the sense of his presence to make us realize our need of him and make us eager to find him again.

The woman's complacency receives a rude jolt: 'My lover had left; he was gone. My heart had gone out to him when he spoke. I looked for him but did not find him. I called him but he did not answer' (v. 6).

A frantic search

The dreamy warmth moves into a frantic search in the cold, dark streets. This passage is, in some ways, a repetition of 3:1–3, but this time there is the additional detail of the beating and robbery. It is possible that the watchmen may be a dramatization of the woman's guilt and fears as she castigates herself, and as frantic blame replaces selfish complacency. Feelings of guilt will not solve the problem, however, since they are simply another example of the self-absorption that causes the difficulties in the first place.

Emotions have been sketched vividly, and at this point the woman speaks frantically to the 'daughters of Jerusalem', who show a way out of the impasse with a challenging question: 'How is your beloved better than others, most beautiful of women? How is your beloved better than others, that you charge us so?' (v. 9).

This takes the emphasis away from both the complacency and the frantic searching, and focuses again on the most basic question of their relationship and its uniqueness.

PRAYER

Lord, when our hearts are cold and our emotions selfish, warm us again by the fire of your love. May we be consistent in our love for you and for each other, in the name of him who loves us and gave himself for us, Jesus Christ our Lord. Amen.

PRAISING

Although this is a new movement, the poem flows smoothly from verse 8 and merges into another love poem or *wasf*. Descriptions of women are common in the Song, as in other ancient love poetry. It is unusual to find such a detailed description of a man, although note similarities with Daniel 10 and Revelation 1. This man is a David-like figure: 'ruddy' is used to describe David in 1 Samuel 16:12 and 17:42, and the phrase is also used of the princes of Israel in Lamentations 4:7.

Good creation

The passage raises a number of both theological and literary issues. The first is the affirmation of the essential goodness of the body. Just as creation is still 'good' even in its fallen state, so is the body, fallen as it is. God himself took a body, and full salvation is seen as a transformation of the body. This belief lies at the very heart of the theology of the Song. The image of God, which is male and female (Genesis 1:26–28), is most fully seen in a loving human couple who, by their mutually harmonious relationship, exemplify the great mystery of love manifest throughout creation.

Effective language

The language blends realism and symbolism. 'His head is purest gold; his hair is wavy and black as a raven' (v. 11) clearly does not mean that he is both dark and blond. Rather, gold (as in vv. 14 and 15) is used to suggest his value. The imagery of gold and jewels is worth comparing with, for example, Daniel 10:5–6 where the 'man' has a belt of purest gold and his body is 'like chrysolite'. In Revelation 1:13–15, the risen Christ has a 'golden sash' and his feet are like bronze.

Some commentators have found these images cold and lifeless, more appropriate for a statue than a human being, but they probably suggest priceless value as well as solid and tangible reality. Moreover, it is important to notice how these solid images are balanced by very different pictures: 'His eyes are like doves by the water streams, washed in milk' (v. 12). Here we have evocations of light and flowing movement, supplemented by the image of perfume in verse 13: 'His cheeks are like beds of spice yielding perfume. His lips are like lilies dripping with myrrh.' The perfume metaphor reminds us of the very beginning of the Song, where the girl, in her dawning passion, longs for a perfumed kiss (1:2–3).

Characteristically, the man is compared with a natural feature, this time with the magnificent cedars of Lebanon (v. 15). This comparison functions somewhat in the same way as the references to Solomon: it creates a sense of magnificence and wonder. It also echoes the honeymoon—'Come with me from Lebanon' (4:8)—and the wood of Solomon's carriage (3:9). Thus there is a combination of solidity and sensitivity, of strength and movement, yet the passage appears to end in anti-climax: 'This is my friend' (v. 16). Friendship, though, is the basis of lasting love. See, for example, Proverbs 17:17: 'A friend loves at all times.' In human terms, romance will have a better chance of lasting if the person you marry is your best friend. On another level, in the midst of profound meditations of love, Jesus said to his disciples, 'You are my friends if you do what I command' (John 15:14).

Reconciliation

The reconciliation after the lovers' tiff continues in 6:1–3, introduced by another question from the friends, who now want to share in the woman's excitement. In verses 2 and 3 we return to the garden imagery and the earliest days of the springtime romance, with all its freshness. The enticing scented atmosphere of the garden contrasts with the bustle and menace of the city. 'Beds of spices' echoes the description of the beloved in 5:13.

Love must be guarded and nourished like a growing garden. Little courtesies, sensitivity, remembering anniversaries and the innumerable acts of kindness are all too easily neglected. This is also true of the relationship with our divine lover: early love can so easily wane. Furthermore, we see that love will not allow itself to be finally lost. Verses 2–3 show that the lover has not gone away permanently, but has withdrawn for a time and then returned to the place of their courtship. Here she echoes 2:16, of the dawning of their love, which she now hopes will be renewed.

PRAYER

Lord, you have made us for love and companionship; help us to be faithful and honest in our relationships. Amen.

LOVE BADE ME WELCOME

The title for this section, taken from George Herbert's poem, breathes the atmosphere of complete acceptance that characterizes these verses. What seems to be happening is that the lovers meet again in the garden. The man speaks words of loving reassurance there, which show that the 'lovers' tiff' of chapter 5 has been forgiven and forgotten and harmony restored. The eyes of the girl are emphasized in verse 5—'Turn your eyes from me; they overwhelm me'—as the man explores something of the depth and resonances of their love.

Love and history

The girl's beauty is compared to two cities whose historical associations are vitally important. Tirzah and Jerusalem (v. 4) represent Israel and Judah, again linking this love story with the great biblical story of God's love for his people. Tirzah was an ancient Canaanite city captured by Joshua (Joshua 12:24). At the time of the division of the kingdom, Jeroboam I made it his capital (1 Kings 14:17), as did his successors until Omri established Samaria (1 Kings 16:23–24). It was a city of groves and gardens, thus reinforcing the garden metaphor. Jerusalem is 'the city of our God, his holy mountain... beautiful in its loftiness, the joy of the whole earth' (Psalm 48:1–2; echoed in Lamentations 2:15). This is not just the love of a shepherd and a shepherdess (although it is that) but the whole biblical drama of God's love for his people, symbolized by their capital cities.

It is worth noting further that ancient Jerusalem was not in itself all that impressive. Many of the psalms speak of 'going up' to Jerusalem, but in strict geographical terms you 'go down' to Jerusalem from the hill country of Judea. The ancient Mount Zion on which stood the Canaanite town taken from the Jebusites by David was an unimpressive little hill. Yet in Psalm 48:2 it is compared to 'the utmost heights of Zaphon', which, in Canaanite myth, was the mountain of the chief god, El, who summoned the other gods to meet there in the divine council. Zaphon fades into insignificance beside Zion, not because of Zion's intrinsic impressiveness but because 'God is in her citadels' (Psalm 48:3). It is transformed by God's love, as, in later days, Athens, Rome and Alexandria would be bypassed in favour of royal David's city. So we have realism and romance, ordinary sight and spiritual vision. God takes us as we are and gradually transforms us into what he wants us to be.

Love and the heavens

This love has cosmic as well as historical dimensions, an idea that emerges in verses 4 and 10: 'majestic as troops with banners... as the stars in procession'. Verse 14 emphasizes the military connotations of the phrase, but the army is probably made up of heavenly bodies (v. 10), part of the army of the Lord of hosts. The word 'majestic' has the nuance of 'terrible, awe-inspiring' and occurs elsewhere in the Old Testament only in reference to the conquering Babylonian armies (see Habakkuk 1:7). This comparison of the girl to the starry heavens widens the picture of young love in chapter 2 as part of the awakening spring landscape. Here it is part of the universe and an anticipation of the time when love will redeem creation.

Love and the future

Love catches up the good things of the past and also points ahead. Hence, verses 5–7 repeat many of the images of 4:2–5 spoken on the wedding night. Now, however, these images are deepened and strengthened by being renewed after misunderstanding and estrangement. Many commentators take verses 8–9 as a reference to Solomon's extensive harem, but the verses are probably using the technique noticed especially in 3:6–11, where the couple's wedding was compared to Solomon's. Here, in contrast to the king's exploitation of women, this man sees this woman as unique.

Verse 10 appears to be their actual meeting, and is introduced by the question 'Who is this?' (compare 3:65, where it introduced the wedding). The imagery of the heavens, anticipated in verse 4, is explicit here. Here, I suggest, the text has deeper mythological overtones, which add a further dimension to the story. Dawn, in Canaanite myth, was a goddess and the other heavenly bodies were objects of veneration. The poet is using the mythological language of Israel's neighbours to underline the cosmic and eternal significance of the events being described.

PRAYER

Lord God, you took Jerusalem and Bethlehem and used them as the places where you touched earth with your love. Transform our ordinary love and make it beautiful by your Spirit. Amen.

SURPRISES *of* LOVE

Who is speaking?

This section is short but beautiful, and contains a number of difficulties. First, it is not entirely clear who is speaking, and translators
and commentators differ in assigning verses 11–12 either to the
woman or to the man. Similar verses are spoken by the woman in
7:12–13, with references to vines and pomegranates. The view taken
here is that these are the words of the woman, who is both recalling
a former meeting and giving a reason for visiting the garden. The
word translated 'grove of nut trees' (v. 11) occurs only here and in
Esther 1:5 and 7:7–8, where it refers to the palace garden.

Overwhelmed by love

Verse 12 is generally considered the most difficult in the book and
detailed notes can be found in larger commentaries. The NIV renders
the text as follows: 'Before I realized it, my desire set me among the
royal chariots of my people.' Alternatively, the second part of the
verse could read 'among the chariots of Amminadab' or 'among the
chariots of the people of the prince'. Literally, the verse reads: 'I
do/did not know, my soul she set me, chariots of Amminadab/people
of the prince.'

Beginning with what is reasonably certain, it seems likely that the
NIV paraphrase 'before I realized it' (echoed in some other versions)
is a reasonable way of understanding the more general 'I did not
know'. The praise of her beauty has transported the girl to the landscape of their honeymoon love and early affection, returned in overwhelming sweetness. The NIV continues with the preposition
'among', which is not in the Hebrew text, but some such word is
needed to link the two parts of the verse.

Chariots are a symbol of royalty—Solomon had 1400 chariots
(1 Kings 10:26)—so this reference reinforces the Solomonic splendour of the couple's relationship. Some commentators want to keep
Amminadab as a proper name, that is, 'chariots of Amminadab'.
Some have suggested that he is the counterpart of Prince Mehy, who,
in Egyptian love lyrics, travels as a royal lover in a chariot. There may

be a slight parallel there, but it does not particularly help our understanding of this verse. Moreover, the rendering 'the royal chariots of my people' fits well with the overall flow of the song. 'My people' is a very common phrase in the Old Testament but, in the overwhelming number of occurrences, it particularly refers to God's love for Israel. Thus the girl is caught up in the great drama of God's love for his people.

Love's dance

Verse 13, given to the friends, suggests that the girl has begun to express her excitement in a dance. Once again this verse is not without its problems. Some see it as an indication that she has already left the garden and the friends want her to return; others suggest that the speakers simply want her to turn and face them. She is here addressed by the otherwise unknown term 'Shulammite', which may well be part of the Solomonic imagery, meaning 'woman of Solomon'. A further question is over the meaning of the 'dance of Mahanaim'. Mahanaim could be a proper name or it could mean 'two camps' or 'two armies'. It could refer to the manner of presentation of the dance, or it may simply be the name of a dance well known then but whose significance is now lost to us.

It is important that these difficulties do not blind us to the obvious issues, however. The first is the creative way in which the couple's renewed love is linked again with new growth, associated in chapter 2 with the spring landscape and the surging of love. 'The new growth in the valley' (v. 11) suggests the association with Abib, a month of spring and ripening, the month in which the Hebrews left Egypt (Exodus 13:4). This may be part of the tapestry of allusions that resulted in the Song being related to the Passover and exodus.

The second issue is that love is mysterious; the very difficulty in translation illustrates why Paul in Ephesians 5:32 describes it as a 'profound mystery'. Ultimately, relationships do not follow strict rules and regulations but are at home in a world of generosity, self-giving, wonder and gratitude.

REFLECTION

It is only by continual gratitude and a sense of wonder that our love will be kept from staleness and selfishness.

LOVE'S DELIGHTS

Now the lover launches into a final *wasf*, which is the culmination of his praise and delight in the attractions of his wife. This *wasf* encapsulates the basic theme of the Song, which is a celebration of humanity made in God's image. It recalls the loving detail of the creator's work in Genesis 1 and 2. Another useful comparison is Psalm 139, with its loving evocation of the intricacy of the human body: 'For you created my inmost being; you knit me together in my mother's womb. I praise you because I am fearfully and wonderfully made; your works are wonderful, I know that full well. My frame was not hidden from you when I was made in the secret place' (Psalm 139:13–15).

Beauty and God's image

Praise of physical beauty is a natural outflow of the belief that humans are in God's image. Such a belief prevents the praise from lapsing into idolatry. Moreover, although the language here is at its most explicit and erotic, it uses vocabulary of a delicate, romantic and symbolic nature. The word translated 'craftsman' (v. 1) occurs only here in the Old Testament, but a related word is used of wisdom in Proverbs 8:30, in a creation context. Both carry suggestions of the delicate and intricate work of the creator, as in Psalm 139.

We would therefore expect that the details of God's creation, as well as the overall plan, would be lovingly carried out. Wine and wheat (v. 2) are symbols of surging life, as are fawns and gazelles (v. 3; also 4:5). Throughout, there is an implied comparison between the human body and the earth itself; just as God looked at creation and pronounced it 'very good', so the human body is good and to be treated with neither revulsion nor idolatry. The language here is realistic, yet transformed by a vision of what the creator has made.

The reality of love

The danger of romantic language is that it can give the impression that there is an unreal quality about love. The poet balances this impression by introducing images of places that emphasize the solid and abiding reality of the couple's love. In verses 4–5, the general comparisons to the beauty of the earth are now more specifically related to the land of Israel and the variety of its life. The limpid pools of Heshbon, another significant city, are used to suggest mystery. Carmel and Lebanon evoke the majesty and durability of mountains.

Plainly, none of this is to be interpreted with crude literalism, but should be seen as colours in an overall picture. This love is not just of the moment; it is part of creation and reflects both the movement of history and the splendour of creation.

The royal nature of love

'Your hair is like royal tapestry; the king is held captive by its tresses. How beautiful you are and how pleasing, O love, with your delights' (vv. 5–6). These words again evoke the theme mentioned several times already, of how their love has transformed this rural couple into royalty in each other's eyes.

The 'king' concludes his praise of the woman with a group of images drawn from plants and trees, which suggest continuing life and growth. The palm tree is noted for its elegant dignity, and the apple tree and its perfume recall the imagery of dawning love in chapters 1 and 2. At the culmination of the poem (v. 9a), the lover echoes the words his bride has used of him in 1:2: 'your mouth like the best wine'.

This remarkable poem has not only shown that the couple's love has been restored but it also points us forward to the final part of the Song, where the timelessness of that love is to be explored.

PRAYER

Our Lord and our great lover, we thank you for catching up our little stories into your great story. May we play our parts in your strength, through Jesus Christ our Lord.

UNDOING *the* CURSE

I have taken this section as beginning at the second part of verse 9, where the girl breaks into her lover's words and takes up his metaphor of wine: 'May the wine go straight to my lover, flowing gently over lips and teeth.' She now speaks until the end of the Song (8:14) and, in my view, is envisaging a kind of second honeymoon, with many echoes of the springtime romance of chapter 2. In particular, the wine reminds her of the first raptures of love, which are now savoured as the relationship matures.

Two things stand out; both are related to the nature of love in the fallen world.

Restoring broken relationships

Verse 10 reads, 'I belong to my lover, and his desire is for me.' These words echo Genesis 3:16: 'Your desire will be for your husband and he will rule over you.' The Genesis passage is part of the judgment pronounced by God as a result of the Fall, yet here the woman gladly uses the phrase to evoke mutual belonging and closeness between them.

The word 'desire' used here occurs in only two other places in the Bible: Genesis 3:16, as already mentioned, and Genesis 4:7, where it is sin that 'desires' to possess Cain. This is a fascinating comparison because what we see in both the Genesis references is how fallen nature seeks to dominate and use power for selfish ends. Here in the Song, however, the 'desire' is that of the lover, which the girl is welcoming. We have already seen that the song is realistic in its depiction of threats to love both from outside and from our own selfish desires. Nevertheless, even in the fallen world, love can partially undo the effects of the Fall. This is underlined by the invitation that Cain gave to Abel in Genesis 4:8. There Cain's motive was evil and selfish and showed that sin had indeed mastered him. Here, in verse 11, the invitation is one of love and mutual longing.

Transformed nature

Love not only restores damaged relationships, however. Love transforms nature itself (vv. 12–13). We saw how the early raptures of love in the springtime of their romance were echoed in the joyful spring-time of the year. Now their renewed love not only looks back to Eden but looks forward to the new heaven and earth (Revelation 21—22).

This poem exists on two levels. On one level it is the landscape of chapter 2, of love's awakening and early dreams, which are being renewed on the second honeymoon at a country retreat. On that level it is a reminder of the need to escape, from time to time, from noise and clutter and to experience God's peace among the beauty of the countryside. On a deeper level, however, it looks to the renewal of creation.

The poet carefully selects details to create the ambience of love and to suggest growth and fragrance. Mandrakes (v. 13) were popularly believed to have aphrodisiac qualities: in Genesis 30:14–16, Leah gives mandrakes to Rachel in return for a night with Jacob. All this is crystallized in the second part of verse 13: 'Over our doors are all choice fruits, new as well as old' (RSV).

True love is always new, but it also transforms the past and every-thing is seen differently as a preparation for that love. It is the same with God's love, which is from all eternity but always has new realms to be explored.

REFLECTION

All of us fail in our relationships, and we need to keep on
renewing our commitments. We need to recover our early love
and to see it mature both through faithfulness in the daily grind
and in romance. To put it another way, we need to share the
domestic chores but we also need candlelit dinners
and special times together.

LOVE *at* HOME

After all these raptures, it comes as something of an anti-climax to hear the girl exclaim, 'O, that you were like a brother to me' (v. 1, RSV). Indeed, for some commentators this verse alone proves that there is no consistent story in the Song and that there has been no marriage; otherwise the woman could scarcely have spoken as she does at this point. I want to suggest that the text can be understood differently. Three factors will help us understand a little more about what this text is saying.

Brother and sister

We have already noticed in 5:16 that the initial ingredient of friend-ship is a love that will last: 'This is my lover, this my friend'. Brother/sister terminology is common in ancient Near Eastern love poetry, and there are examples from both Canaan and Egypt. Genesis 2:24 speaks of a man and woman becoming 'one flesh', which means, among other things, that marriage has created a new organic relationship like that of people born into the same family. Here in the Song, the same idea is suggested by the use of the word 'brother'. No one word or concept can exhaust the rich and growing nature of this relationship. The kiss (v. 1) links this passage with chapter 1, where the relationship began. It is a characteristic of the Song, which has often been noted already, that earlier images, ideas and situations are taken up again later, and this serves to emphasize the developing nature of love.

Love's teaching

Love is spontaneous, yet it can be learned: '… and bring you to my mother's house—she who has taught me' (v. 2). There is a textual point here. The NIV and other versions have the mother as the teacher, but the form of the verb could suggest the second person masculine—that is, '*you* who taught me', referring to the lover. It is more likely to mean the mother, because it echoes 3:4, which talked of the girl's conception. However, the ambiguity may be deliberate. Her mother has already given her instruction, and now her lover is to continue the process. This instruction is not mere theory: the wine and the pomegranates (v. 2) give it a tangible reality, reinforced by verse 3: 'His left arm is under my head and his right arm embraces me.' Verse 3 also echoes 2:6, where the phrase evokes the rapture of the dawning love; here it links to the deeper raptures of a mature and still maturing relationship.

The 'friends' bow out

For the last time, the woman speaks the refrain, 'Daughters of Jerusalem, I charge you: Do not arouse or awaken love until it so desires' (v. 4). This warning has already been spoken in 2:7 and 3:5, serving as a reminder that love is powerful and consuming and that it must not be forced. But this love has taken its natural course. It has triumphed over the effects of the Fall, and has matured in the world of domesticity. Now it is to face the severest test of all.

The final words of the friends (v. 5a) echo 3:6 and suggest that, for the lovers, the desert experience is over and that they are enjoying full intimacy.

PRAYER

Lord of yesterday, today and for ever, kindle and maintain in us the love that never fails. Amen.

LOVE IS STRONGER *than* DEATH

This lyric is one of the most powerful in the Song and is arguably the very heart of its theological and literary emphases. It is introduced by the question already foreshadowed in 3:6: 'Who is this coming up from the desert leaning on her lover?' We previously noted the potent symbolism of the desert and its overtones of discipline and dependence (see p. 148). Here the desert is juxtaposed with the apple tree and all its life-giving associations. These opposites are a clever introduction to the lyric that follows. The tree, with its vibrant energy, is a symbol of love as it contends with destructive elemental forces.

Sealed by love

A cluster of images is introduced in verse 6 by the seal. In the ancient world, people of standing wore their own personal seals either on a cord around their necks or as rings on their fingers. In Haggai 2:23 Zerubbabel is said by God to be his signet ring, showing that he is God's special possession. Here the seal emphasizes the exclusive nature of the relationship between the man and woman. In Ephesians 1:13, the Spirit is the sign and seal that God's loving purposes will be fulfilled.

Love defeats death

Throughout the Song, love has been threatened by many enemies: the little foxes (2:15), the desert (3:6), the violence of the watchmen (5:7). Now the great elemental forces of love and death meet face to face. Here the story of a shepherd boy and his beloved is most clearly an embodiment of that great love story which is the drama of the universe itself; the threatening forces are not simply domestic tragedies but the awesome powers of darkness and chaos.

There are many passages in the Old Testament where death is personified, and there are echoes of Canaanite myth where Baal battles with and eventually overcomes Mot, god of death. Some examples are Psalm 49:14: 'death will feed on them'; and Hosea 13:14: 'Where, O death, are your plagues? Where, O grave, is your destruction?' The 'jealousy' (better, 'ardour' or 'passion') of love is the only power that can master the abode of the dead. At the very heart of the great drama of God's love for the world is the story of how death, at its most savage, flung its forces against love incarnate and was defeated.

Love and God's presence

'It burns like blazing fire, like a mighty flame' (v. 6b). Fire is associated with the presence of God: the blazing sword at the gates of Eden (Genesis 3:24), the smoke of Mount Sinai (Exodus 19:18), and the fiery chariot (2 Kings 2:11) are some examples. The phrase 'like a mighty flame' could be rendered 'like a flame of Yahweh', which would make it the only specific reference to God in the Song. Perhaps the nearest we could come to the idea in English is the expression 'a divine flame'. Here we have evoked the awesome presence and power of God.

Love conquers chaos

The 'many waters' and rivers' (v. 7) again have a mythological background: in Canaanite myth, Baal battles with the powers of the sea god. This is reflected in other Old Testament passages where the God of Israel conquers the sea: for example, Psalm 93:4: 'Mightier than the thunder of the great waters, mightier than the breakers of the sea—the Lord on high is mighty.' The waters in the Song are the cosmic powers of evil that dog the progress of love. But nothing in the universe is stronger than love.

Love and money

The second part of verse 7 seems an anti-climax, and some commentators have dismissed it as trite moralizing: 'If one were to give all the wealth of his house for love, it would be utterly scorned.' However, it is a striking reminder that love is the most vital force in the universe and cannot be bought. It is no more at the mercy of market forces than it is the plaything of cosmic powers. If our lives are not lived in the realm of love, then no success and no glittering prizes can compensate for that lack.

REFLECTION

Think about your priorities. Are they driven by love or by some lesser consideration?

A CURTAIN CALL

Many commentators express dissatisfaction with what they see as the fragmentary and disjointed nature of these final verses, but I want to suggest that they are a kind of curtain call where various characters and images bow out. The immediate connection is that the poet has just shown the absurdity of imagining that love is a commercial product; yet in the next verses we have people who do just that.

Two ways of getting it wrong

Who is speaking in verses 8–10? It could be the brothers themselves, or it could be the woman quoting them. Since most of this final section is spoken by her, I think it likely that she is quoting rather than that new speakers are introduced at this late stage. And who is the sister? It may be the woman's younger sister, who is not yet physically mature. However, these verses could be a flashback to the woman's own earlier experience, and the use of the first person in verse 10 supports this view.

We have already noticed the rather boorish behaviour of the woman's brothers (1:6). Verses 8–9 could be taken as a expression of care and concern by them, but there is probably a negative tone. Following on from verse 7b with its commercial metaphor, the images of the wall and door, and the luxurious nuances of cedar and silver, evoke a mean-spirited mentality that regards a woman as part of a man's disposable property. The brothers think they can keep her chaste with rules and regulations and by hiding her away.

She responds with a strong and vigorous independence (v. 10). Love, far from crushing her personality, has allowed it to grow and mature. She has no need of petty rules and regulations symbolized by walls and doors. Love, which is stronger than death and the mighty waters, cannot be confined by artificial barriers. So one way of dealing wrongly with love is by surrounding it with restrictive regulations.

Verses 11 and 12 are puzzling, but, in my view, they describe another way of treating a woman as disposable property: with lechery and prostitution. The reappearance of Solomon is unexpected, but perhaps the 'vineyard' stands for his harem. Baal Hamon is not otherwise known, although a god of that name is mentioned in

Carthaginian inscriptions. It may have been a place where Solomon's twin activities of philandering and worshipping pagan gods took place. His vast wealth may have bought him many vineyards, but one vineyard is not his. This girl cannot be bought; she is for her lover alone (v. 12).

These verses have evoked again the threats and dangers to love. This Song, so romantic and beautiful, shows a painful awareness of the fact that love must work itself out in an imperfect and threatening world.

More to come

The book is to end on a positive and exultant note, with the lovers face to face and in conversation with each other. The last words of the man are full of longing to hear the woman (v. 13) and she invites him to further intimacy (v. 14), using language similar to 2:17 as the curtain falls. The Song, which began with the story already in motion, ends on an unfinished note. Many commentators have found this unsatisfactory, but it could scarcely be bettered. Love never ends; what we have swum is only a tributary of the great river, only an anticipation of further delights.

We have tried to understand the Song in its wider biblical context. In that context, this story of a long-dead man and woman nevertheless shows that love is stronger than death because it will outlast it and indeed destroy it. Thus Paul exults, 'The last enemy to be destroyed is death' (1 Corinthians 15:26). Because love has already given the fatal blow to death by the cross and resurrection, we know that, in spite of our own weakness and vulnerability, we will share in that victory.

That is why, in our study of the Song, we have tried to do justice both to its human and divine dimensions. We have tried not to extract allegorical significance from every detail but to show how this human love mirrors a love greater than itself. The Song of Songs is no mere byway of scripture but is at the heart of what the Bible is about.

REFLECTION

Jesus, the very thought of thee with sweetness fills the breast,
But sweeter far thy face to see, and in thy presence rest.
O hope of every contrite heart, O joy of all the meek,
To those who fall, how kind thou art, how good to those who seek.

Bernard of Clairvaux

GIVING GRIEF *a* VOICE

Five lyrics, each of them saying in different ways that life is bleak and harsh, seem unpromising material from which to gain spiritual nourishment. Yet the little book of Lamentations has important lessons for us, and addresses issues of grief and suffering that we dare not ignore.

Occasion and author

The occasion for these lyrics is the destruction of Jerusalem in 587BC and the grim reality of exile in Babylon. The author is one of the few who were not deported, and he mourns over the ruins and asks big questions about why it has happened and what it has done to the faith of Israel. The Hebrew Bible does not name an author, and it is the Greek translation that first attributes the book to Jeremiah: 'After the captivity of Israel and the destruction of Jerusalem, Jeremiah sat weeping and composed this lament saying...' reads 1:1 of that version. In 2 Chronicles 35:25, Jeremiah is said to have written laments for Josiah, which continued to be recited by singers. However, the absence of any mention of Josiah in Lamentations makes it likely that the Chronicler is referring to a composition now lost. In any case, plural forms are used of the speakers in chapters 4 and 5; in chapters 1 and 2 the personified Jerusalem speaks, as well as an anonymous individual in chapter 3. The book as a whole speaks for the exiles. The Hebrew text makes no mention of an author, so we are probably to regard it as the voice of the community, crystallized by an unknown poet.

Its value

Like the lament psalms, Job and much of Jeremiah, Lamentations raises in an acute form the problem of suffering. This is reinforced by the literary form of the book, which is one of the most highly organized in the Old Testament. The poems are acrostics, following the sequence of the Hebrew alphabet. This gives us, in effect, an *Aleph* to *Yaw* or, as we would say, an A to Z, of suffering. There is a long road to be travelled; grief must be lived through and the process cannot be short-circuited. As we shall see, the depths of human suffering and the way we speak of them to the Lord are the subject of this book.

Its use

Like the other books that make up the Five Scrolls, Lamentations plays its part in the ancient Jewish liturgical year (see Introduction, p. 11). It was used on the 9th of Ab, the fifth month of the Jewish calendar, to commemorate the destruction of the temple by Nebuchadnezzar, and also in later centuries the destruction of the second temple by Titus in AD70. This was a penitential season, not unlike Lent, and Lamentations is an important biblical witness to the sinfulness of humanity and the cost of forgiving that sin. Unlike some of the other scrolls, the canonicity of Lamentations was never questioned.

In the first two verses, some important guidelines for understanding the book are laid down. The first is the description of Jerusalem as a widow. Widows in the ancient world were particularly vulnerable because there was no social security and they were totally dependent on other members of the family to support them. If she is a widow, then who was her husband? We know from the Old Testament that he was none other than Yahweh himself. We know, too, that he is not dead, so the idea that he has abandoned her is at the heart of her lamentation. Moreover, we know that he has abandoned her because of her unfaithfulness, underlined by the word 'lovers' in verse 2. In Ezekiel 16, the prophet retells the history of Israel as a love story in which the bride turns prostitute. Jerusalem here in Lamentations is not simply the city but represents the whole of God's people.

The second guideline is the numbing sense of a fall from former greatness. Jerusalem was queen and great among the nations (v. 1)— probably referring to the days of David and Solomon (with a reminder of how Solomon himself sank down into unfaithfulness). The glowing words of the 'Zion psalms' such as Psalm 48, as well as Isaiah 2 and Micah 4, also portray a glorious future for Jerusalem as the centre of the redeemed earth. What will happen to that promise now?

Lament is an essential part of the life of faith. All Christians will hurt, and sometimes hurt badly. We need to learn a language in which we can honestly bring our hurts and griefs to God and question the suffering. Our study of Lamentations will provide us with insights into that very matter.

PRAYER

Lord, teach us to pray when praying is hard, and to wrestle with our pain and questions. Amen.

The EMPTY ROADS

The poet now describes the situation that gave rise to the book. The situation is first seen from the outside, looking in. In a number of vivid pictures, he outlines the distress of the ruined city.

Divine judgment

The author is in no doubt why the catastrophe has happened: 'The Lord has brought her grief because of her many sins' (v. 5). This is very different from the book of Job, where the author wrestles with the problem of undeserved suffering. Job emphasizes the main character's innocence of specific sins leading to the disasters that overtake him, but in Lamentations the link between sin and suffering is clear. Books such as Job warn us that not all suffering is a result of specific sin, but sometimes it is, and the exile is a clear case in point.

Human sinfulness

Sin is seen in verses 8–9 primarily in terms of uncleanness. 'Nakedness' and 'filthiness' are often closely associated with ritual impurity (for example, in Leviticus 18:19). Judah has become ceremonially unclean and unfit for the holiness of God. Similar language is used elsewhere in the Old Testament to describe the humiliation of conquered nations (for example, Isaiah 47:3; Jeremiah 13:26). The word translated 'sins' in verse 5 would be more accurately rendered 'rebellions', and this comes close to the heart of the book's theology. What has happened is no accident. It is not ultimately the Babylonian armies that have done the damage; it is the punishment for Jerusalem's rebellion. The question here is not, as in Job, the mystery of suffering unrelated to sin. Rather, sin is admitted, and the question is, 'What now?'

The atmosphere

Judgment and sin are themes that can be dealt with in a variety of ways, some tough and some tender. The way in which this author deals with them is by imagery. Pictures are created, showing the one devastating event of the exile from different angles. Notice the family relationship implied in the phrase 'daughter of Zion' (v. 6). Zion's sins are sins against her true family identity. She has lost her status and her privileges. This means that, while there is no attempt to hide her sinfulness, the tone is one of lament and regret rather than condemnation and recrimination. Condemnation is to come, but it is important to realize that it comes in the context of estranged relationship rather than in an impersonal legalistic setting. Something valuable has gone, and this is underlined by the use of such words as 'splendour' (v. 6) and 'treasures' (vv. 7, 10, 11). This latter word could refer to the people, not simply possessions, highlighting the covenantal emphasis of this section.

Other images, such as the deer (v. 6) and wandering (v. 7), are not to be taken literally but are metaphors of vulnerability and alienation, giving different perspectives on the experience of exile. The author is using the language and style of funeral liturgies here and throughout the book, to emphasize the deeply personal nature of the event: it is a bereavement. This is merged with the language of confession, which begins to point to a possible way forward—an increasingly important theme as the book progresses.

Lamentations raises hard questions about the people's relationship with God. Jerusalem/Zion is the centre of God's glory in Psalms such as 46, 48 and 122, and the sign of his favour. What will happen now, not only to God's people but to God's honour and his promises? This is the huge question with which the exilic and post-exilic literature of the Old Testament wrestles.

It is important not to try to gloss over the issues here and adopt a cavalier attitude to the situation. What has happened in the exile is a huge question mark over the whole history of God's people and over the covenant with Abraham, Moses and David. Lamentations is an uncomfortable book, and yet it is one of the most powerful and moving articulations in the Old Testament of grief and lament.

REFLECTION

Examine your hymn books and see how much in them helps us to voice feelings of pain and sinfulness.

A VIEW *from the* INSIDE

The first part of this chapter was largely a description of how the
ruined Jerusalem appeared from the outside. Now we turn to a view
from the inside as the city personified 'speaks' for itself. Here we have
a more personal and, in some ways, more theological view of the
event.

The nature of the event

A casual reader might well miss the point of these verses. After all, the
fall of a city in the ancient world, with all its accompanying horrors,
was not a rare event and we know only too well that the tragedies of
war and violence are no less severe in the contemporary world. The
difference here, however, is that this is an apocalyptic event—one
foreshadowing the end of the world. This is the day of 'the Lord's
fierce anger' (v. 12) This is the day of wrath of which the prophet
Zephaniah speaks (Zephaniah 1:14—2:3), and the image is reinforced by the references to fire, which remind us of God's blazing
holiness first seen at the gates of Eden, barring the way back to the
tree of life (Genesis 3:24). Here the fire is from heaven and it is all-
consuming ('sent it down into my bones', v. 13). The fall of the city
is not simply the result of warfare; it is punishment from God. God
is further seen as a hunter (v. 13) who ensnares people in his net
(compare Hosea 7:12), and as a man who tramples a winepress
(v. 15; compare Isaiah 63:3–4).

However, verse 12 with its reference to unsurpassed sorrow has
often been held to have a deeper meaning. The true son of God is to
suffer in this very place, both as a result of the unfaithfulness of his
people and as an answer to that unfaithfulness. At the cross, God's
love and anger come together. The words of this verse in the
Authorized Version have been immortalized in Handel's *Messiah*:
'Behold and see'.

The theology of the event

Much of Lamentations uses imagery to convey powerfully the inner
meaning of the fall of Jerusalem. Sometimes, however, the author
moves directly into theology, and verses 18–22 are one such passage.

Here he begins, in the form of a prayer, to grapple with the issues. First he recognizes God's integrity: 'The Lord is righteous.' In this situation God is the innocent party and his people are guilty. This admission is accompanied by the recognition that all human help is gone (v. 19) and that there is no help other than in the Lord, who is the injured party. This is painful to realize, but only in such a realization is there any hope of beginning to rebuild the relationship. It is out of such anguish that a new community is to be formed so that the story may continue through and beyond exile. The poet admits the guilt of the people—'I have been most rebellious' (v. 20)—and by doing so begins to move the situation on.

A wider question is addressed in verses 21 and 22, which look at judgment on Israel's neighbours. This is the theme of the little book of Obadiah, which castigates Edom both for mockery and malevolence during the Babylonian siege of Jerusalem. Similar strictures on Babylon occur in Isaiah 47. The theme is not particularly developed in Lamentations, but it is present, and it is a reminder of the theology of God and the nations that we find in many of the prophets. When they speak of other nations, the prophets see them as also responsible to the one true God, who will judge them as well as Israel.

This is not a full theology of suffering and sin. We have to range more widely through the Bible in the writings of such prophets as Isaiah and Jeremiah, in the lament and penitential psalms and in Job, as well as in narratives such as the David/Bathsheba story in 2 Samuel 11—12. Above all, we will need to meditate on the story of the cross and the apostolic commentary on that event. However, in Lamentations we do have a powerful presentation of suffering and a genuine confession of sin. The language is poetic and deliberately so. Only such words are adequate to convey the powerful and all-but-overwhelming emotions. Thus we cannot press precise details and must, rather, see how the details build up into a overall picture. More importantly, there is a determination to engage with God and see how he will respond.

REFLECTION

In the terrible grief of the children of Sudan, in the hopeless despair
of their families and the apparently unending nature of their
suffering, we can see something of the same sorrow.

LIKE *an* ENEMY

A superficial reading would suggest that all the chapters of this book are saying the same thing. It is true that the same subject is being dealt with, but neither in the same way nor with exactly the same emphases. Chapter 1 dealt more specifically with 'what'—that is, exile and especially the destruction of the city. Here, the poem moves on, and there is more emphasis on 'why'.

The anger of God

'The cloud of his anger' is mentioned in verse 1, with 'fierce anger' in verses 3 and 6, and this is the driving force behind the events. The 'cloud' in the exodus story was the sign of God's protection and guidance in the desert (for example, Exodus 13:21; 14:19–20), but now the cloud is angry and threatening. 'Fierce anger' suggests its reality and passion. The anger of God, unlike ours, never springs from injured vanity, and it is always related to his love. He cares passionately about his people and will not allow them less than the best. God's anger is an integral part of the gospel, and a God who cannot be angry is also a God incapable of love. Clearly a line has been crossed and God is punishing his people. An earlier prophet, Amos, was told not to intercede for Israel any longer as they had passed the point of no return (Amos 7:7–9).

The contrast with the past

These verses have many echoes of earlier scriptures, which speak of God's favour and protection and underline the contrast with the situation here. We have already noticed how the cloud now turns a dark side to the people (as it once did to the Egyptians: Exodus 14:20). Further, the 'Zion psalms' are turned on their head here. Far from being a place where God himself is its 'fortress' (Psalm 46:7), the city is now a ruin. Far from pondering the security that comes from God and is told to the next generation (Psalm 48:12–14), the people have seen God himself sending enemies to destroy the city. The 'appointed feasts and Sabbaths' are set aside (v. 6) because they celebrate God's loving provision as creator and the greatness of his salvation, especially in the exodus, and now this seems no longer valid. God is an archer (vv. 4–5), unleashing judgment as once he sent the flood. In Genesis 9:13–17, after the flood, God laid aside the bow, but now he takes it up.

There is a profound lesson in all this. God chose Israel, but she proved to be interested only in privilege, and careless of responsibility. Lamentations reminds us in the privileged and 'post-Christian' West of the danger of presumption and of forgetting God's demand for holiness and integrity. Church history is littered with examples of once-flourishing churches, and even whole denominations, that have disappeared because of unfaithfulness. None of us is indispensable to God, and we need to hear this.

The broken relationship

Perhaps most poignantly, God 'has not remembered his footstool' (v. 1). The 'footstool' is a more specific image than the city, even than the temple, and stands for the ark of the covenant (in 1 Chronicles 28:2 it is explicitly said to be God's footstool). This is the place where God met with his people and graciously forgave their sins. All the other calamities follow on from the abandonment of this meeting place. If the basic relationship with God is broken, then nothing else will be right. Not only is the city destroyed but the whole fabric of life has vanished (v. 9). The political infrastructure is no more; worse, the Torah is neglected and the prophets no longer speak messages from God. Leadership at all levels has failed utterly and has been judged for that failure.

We need to ponder deeply on what this chapter is saying. Many remedies are suggested to heal the dryness of so much of today's church life, and many of these suggestions are good and helpful. However, we seem reluctant to face the possibility that God may be judging us and calling us to repentance. This is not to suggest a naive one-to-one comparison between the world of 586BC and that of today. Rather, it is to say that we must honestly face the possibility of judgment and wrestle with its implications. If a relationship is broken, it will not be mended by platitudes and emotional discourse; a book like Lamentations uses powerful language and vivid imagery as it tries to find a way back to God in the darkness.

REFLECTION

Repentance is a vital part of the life of faith and we need to be
willing to be utterly open and honest with God.

A DESPERATE CRY

Here the author uses the first person again, moving from description to an inside view of the experience. This switching from description to an inside view and back again is one of the features that gives the book its emotional appeal and helps us to approach the situation from a number of perspectives. The author is caught up in tragic events. He is reliving the horror of the fall of Jerusalem and paints a grim picture of starving children and streets piled with bodies. The destruction of Jerusalem by the Babylonian armies brought an end to the independent existence of Judah and began the period known as the exile (see 2 Kings 25). The contemporary world sees many such horrors from famine-devastated Africa.

The Lord's judgment

'The Lord has done what he planned; he has fulfilled his word, which he decreed long ago. He has overthrown you without pity' (v. 17). This is the basic theological conviction of the author about the exile. Whatever the secondary causes may have been, it was the Lord who caused the devastation. Neither was the decision arbitrary; it had long been predicted by such prophets as Amos (5:18–20) and, more recently, by Zephaniah (1:14–18). They had spoken of the darkness and distress of the 'day of the Lord'. Deuteronomy 28 and 1 Kings 8 had also spelled out the consequences of rebellion, which were now being fulfilled. Much of the blame is directed at false prophets who have failed in their duty of exposing the people's sinfulness. They have offered bogus comfort and failed to call for repentance (v. 14).

The call to prayer

Verse 18 is an important turning point in the chapter: 'The hearts of the people cry out to the Lord.' The recognition that the Lord has punished them drives them not to despair but to the realization that the only one who can help is the one who has condemned them. This is a further reminder that, until the relationship with the Lord is put right, everything else will go wrong. Restoring the relationship is no mere formality: it is more important than sleep, and its outward sign is tears poured out like a river (v. 19).

The final verses, with their grim picture of cannibalism caused by famine, are part of the prayer and an appeal to the compassion of God. This prayer contains real bitterness, and our author is not afraid to share his feelings with God.

This chapter is not comfortable reading; indeed, this whole book must be one of the most neglected in the entire Bible because of its harrowing tone. It is a powerful reminder that tragedy of this nature is not amenable to smart answers and easy situations. We are probably not in the same situation, but if we are suffering the effects of one like it, we are given words to help us to wrestle with its deeper meaning. God is regularly called 'Lord' here, which reminds us of his covenant relationship with his people. This must be placed beside the sickening reality of what is happening, as we wrestle with the deeper meaning of the event.

The covenant relationship is reinforced by the poetic language used. The echoes of the Psalms, already noted, increase the sense of alienation, with all their associations of a way of life that has gone. Now there is no temple where the Psalms can be sung, and their hauntingly beautiful words seem to be a mockery. The language of Lamentations is frank and honest, and that in itself can be a sign of moving on. Only by total honesty can the broken relationship with God be restored. It is not through merely rational and passionless words that damaged relationships can be mended. There will be pain, tears and strong language before a new way forward can be found. That way forward is going to be the subject of the next chapter.

REFLECTION

In the day of my trouble I seek the Lord; in the night my hand is stretched out without wearying; my soul refuses to be comforted. I think of God, and I moan; I meditate, and my spirit faints.

Psalm 77:2–3 (RSV)

NO HOPE LEFT

We come now to the longest and most complex of the five lyrics that make up the book, and this is reflected in its pattern. We have noted that the poems are acrostics. More specifically, chapters 1—2 and 4—5 each have 22 verses beginning with the letters of the Hebrew alphabet, while in chapter 3 the pattern is more elaborate: there are 66 verses made up of 22 stanzas of three verses, each of which begins with a letter of the Hebrew alphabet. Moreover, this chapter is dominated by personal references in which the poet-commentator identifies himself with the city of Zion and takes up its lament. Chapter 3 contains some of the most despairing language of the book, as well as its greatest leap of faith. We may therefore compare it with Job 19:13–27, which begins in the depth of despair and yet contains the amazing vision of the redeemer who lives. Another comparison with Job is that, just as that book moves far beyond the suffering of the main character to suffering in general, so here the author moves from the specific situation of the fall of Jerusalem to the huge issues of God's providence and disaster. Much of the language is reminiscent of Job's speeches and the personal urgency is unmistakable.

The poet's identification with Zion

Some commentators have argued that the speaker here cannot be the poet assuming the persona of Zion because of the first person plural in 3:40, but if the book is read as a whole it seems most likely that this is the poet deliberately identifying with the people. The author of Hebrews (4:15–16) speaks of Jesus as one who is able to sympathize with our weakness, and this is an anticipation of that identification. The poet is providing a voice for the community to crystallize their deepest feelings and, furthermore, because of the lack of specific reference to the fall of Jerusalem, he is providing a voice for all who find themselves in comparable circumstances. Once again the language is powerful and probing.

God's role

God is not a passive spectator; he is using the enemies of his people to punish his people for their sins. Once again this is shown very effectively by echoing earlier scriptures that speak of God's mercy and protection. Verse 1 is very close to Job 9:34 and 21:9; verse 2 to Job 19:8; and verse 7 to Job 7:18. Then there are the stark contrasts: in Psalm 23 God leads his people into life, but here he leads them into darkness (v. 2). Instead of rescuing them from Egyptian slavery, he has consigned them to Babylonian chains (v. 7). Instead of giving protection against 'the arrow that flies by day' (Psalm 91:5), he himself has become the archer (vv. 12–13). The fundamental issue is not simply suffering in itself, but what that suffering does to the ancient belief in God which had been the very *raison d'être* for this community.

It is important not to fudge the issue. The apparent hostility of God is a huge problem, yet nowhere is there any suggestion that abandoning him will make things better. Indeed, it was abandoning him that had led to this situation. Rather, there is a wrestling with God, holding up the problem to him and refusing to let go. This is an invaluable reminder to us that other people have wrestled with the mystery of God's providence and found themselves pushed to the very limit. This struggle has not been edited out of the Bible, but has been left for all future generations, in words that give us a voice in situations of darkness.

PRAYER

Lord, give us honesty in our prayers. May we never try to hide our sorrows from you. Amen.

New Every Morning

In one sense, nothing has changed; yet, like a train leaving a long dark tunnel and emerging into the sunlight, we move into a brighter and calmer landscape. The poet realizes that no help can come, apart from the one who sent the judgment.

Remembering past blessings

The 'hope' in verse 21 is not an attempt to evade the miserable realities of the present, but rather an act of faith built on the character of God as already revealed in the past. The poet does not ask God for an explanation; rather, he turns to the certainties of the character of God. He has called on God to 'remember' (3:19, RSV), which is, in effect, a call on God to act: when God remembers, he acts decisively (Genesis 8:1). This is paralleled (3:20) with the poet's own remembering, which is what leads to hope. A sober realization of what has gone wrong is a necessary condition for beginning the process of putting it right.

Content of this hope

Now follow the positive and beautiful verses that are the high point of the whole book (vv. 22–24). The poet is beginning to look to the future. The great realities of the covenant that God made with his people are now recalled. The 'great love' of the Lord translates the Hebrew word *hesed*, which is the particular term used to refer to the love God has pledged to his people. It is not mere kindness; it is the passionate and unconditional love whereby God commits himself with promises that he cannot and will not break. Most significantly, this is the love that God showed in Exodus 32—34, when his people rebelled against him in the incident of the golden calf (see Exodus 34:6–7). His 'compassions', or 'mercies', emphasize parental concern, and the word in the singular can mean 'womb'. 'Portion' is used of a tract of land given to each of the tribes of Israel (for example, Joshua 19:9); and in Numbers 18:20 it is used of the spiritual inheritance of the priests, which is to be God himself. This means that the poet can now come to terms with the loss of Jerusalem.

The nature of God

Verse 25–27 are more reflective, and the poet claims his own experience for others. This section is dominated by the word 'good', and in Hebrew each of the verses begins with that word. We have moved well beyond the specific situation of the fall of Jerusalem, to consider the nature of God and a good relationship with him, and the educative value of suffering, like a yoke keeping oxen from going astray (v. 27). It is good to act directly—to 'seek'—as well as to wait patiently 'for the salvation of the Lord'. Waiting is not simply marking time; it is an attitude of positive expectation that God will work.

Verses 28–30 reflect more clearly the specific situation of the book, showing that spirituality can never be divorced from who and where we are.

God's overall purpose

What has been said is now related to the continuing character of God and his loving purposes (vv. 31–36). Suffering is never an end in itself and ultimately must lead to joy. This realization will save us from a kind of pseudo-spirituality that tries to give suffering an intrinsic rather than an educative value. God will and does punish, notably in the exile, because his people are sinful, but he does it for the greater good of those so afflicted. The cruelty to prisoners and the flouting of justice that were characteristic of the exile (vv. 34–36) are not pleasurable to the Lord, who is nevertheless using this experience to bring about ultimate blessing.

The section is rounded off in verses 37–39 with the affirmation that God is behind everything good and bad, and that, while judgment comes from him, it is also only from him that relief and blessing can come. This idea is crystallized in verse 39 as 'punishment for sins'. What needs to be lamented is our sinfulness, and that introduces us to the next section.

PRAYER

Lord, help us to see beyond outward events
and to trust in your goodness. Amen.

TEARS *of* REPENTANCE

Repentance is often confused with feelings of sorrow. There will certainly be such feelings if there is genuine repentance, but repentance is fundamentally an entire change of attitude, in ways that are helpfully spelled out for us in this section.

What does it mean?

Repentance means, first of all, self-examination. We cannot truly repent if we do not 'examine our ways and test them' (v. 40). This is necessary for us before we can 'return' to the Lord, and it is a continual call from the prophets. There must be genuine prayer, often symbolized by the lifting of hands (v. 41; see Psalms 28:2; 63:4), but this must not be merely an outward show. 'Hearts' as well as hands must be involved. There must be confession of sin, seeing it as God sees it—as 'transgression and rebellion' (v. 42). This is not a mechanical series of steps, but a picture of true repentance.

The content of the prayer

Verses 42–47 are cast in the form of a communal prayer, which embodies the repentance of the people and calls on the God who has punished them, to rescue them. The necessity of repentance is powerfully underlined in verse 42: 'you have not forgiven'. God's forgiveness is not cheap grace; it is a costly and painful process. The harsh reality of slaughter, mockery and hatred from the nations, and the sense of loss, are as bitter as ever. Once again the cloud hides God rather than protecting his people. Prayer cannot, it seems, penetrate that cloud (v. 44). The absence of God is overwhelming, and yet the writer refuses to let go. Indeed, in verse 48, he reverts to the first person singular because of the overwhelming nature of his emotion, and he moves into lament form, with an emphasis on his tears.

He is again concerned for the sorrows of the desolate city and for the grief of the others, especially the women of the city. But 'women' or 'daughters' of the city (v. 51) could also mean the other towns of Judah, which are seen as daughters of Zion. In either case, the sorrow is evident.

These are important verses, following as they do the lyrical thanksgiving section, and the two parts have deliberately been placed together to provide balancing truths. The mercy of God is a constant and unwavering aspect of his nature and is not set aside because of tragic and mysterious circumstances. At the same time, judgment and punishment of sin are also part of his character. This means that we should neither take his goodness for granted, nor despair at his judgment.

The force of the prayer

The switch between the singular and plural shows that this is no mere outsider's view. The poet identifies with the people. He is going through the same experience and thus can speak for them. He knows the huge problems of reconciling what he believes with the circumstances in which he finds himself. This interplay of the communal and the personal is at the heart of much biblical theology. We live in a very individualistic society and often find it difficult to think and feel in communal terms, especially in the language of grief.

Moreover, the powerful emotion here is a reminder that our often passionless and uninvolved approach to our faith makes it difficult for us to handle such tragic and cataclysmic events as the exile. Scripture is full of emotion, sometimes bitter and desolate emotion such as this, and its presence gives us words and images to help express our own darker emotions.

Furthermore, there is the sense that there are no quick fixes: '...until the Lord looks down from heaven and sees' (v. 50). This expresses the sense of waiting on the Lord and praying that he will act. The image of the Lord looking down from heaven is common in the Old Testament. Sometimes it has nuances of blessing (for example, Deuteronomy 26:15) and sometimes of judgment (for example, Psalm 14:2). Probably here the author is both remembering how the Lord has looked down in judgment and hoping for that look to become one of blessing.

PRAYER

The words of Habakkuk 3:2 form a prayer that speaks directly to the situation here:

'Lord, I have heard of your fame; I stand in awe of your deeds, O Lord. Renew them in our day, in our time make them known; in wrath remember mercy.'

Asking God *to* Judge

Now the poet returns to his own situation, which is also the situation of the city and is concerned powerfully with the theological implications of what has happened.

Calling on his name

Two metaphors are used to evoke the poet's sense of vulnerability and hopelessness. A hunting metaphor (v. 52) has already been used in 1:13, and it suggests the relentlessness of the enemy. The 'pit' represents more than just imprisonment; this is one of the words used of *Sheol* (the underworld), and the exile is indeed a world of death without apparent hope of resurrection. Like Jonah, the poet feels submerged and, like Jonah, he calls on the Lord. Now he is discovering God's answer even in the worst of circumstances. There is a fascinating glimpse into the nature of prayer in verses 55–57. The prayer, in one sense, causes God to answer: 'You came near when I called you'. Given the depths of the experience, however, he is able to pray only because God has moved him to do so. Prayer is a relationship, and here the relationship has gone through the most intense suffering.

Calling on him to judge

The poet, rather like Job in chapter 19, calls on God to vindicate him, to carry out vengeance on his enemies. This raises in an acute way the problem of judgment. So far, the poet has freely confessed that the exile was a justly deserved punishment and a result of the people's sin. Here he is making a different point. God's punishment is one thing, but those whom God has used to punish his people have far exceeded their brief (vv. 60–63). It is one thing to be an instrument in God's hand, carrying out his judgment; it is quite another to delight in cruelty and to treat with hatred and contempt the objects of that judgment. A similar idea occurs in Habakkuk 2:4–17 where the Babylonians are castigated for their excessive severity. Now, for the first time, the author begins to call on God to judge those who have brought about this situation. He sees the enemies as enemies primarily of God, and thus as opponents of his loving purposes.

The language used

We have already noticed how sometimes the language used in Lamentations resembles that of the Psalms. In this passage, it is particularly the language of the imprecatory or cursing Psalms (for example, Psalm 137). These psalms are hard, and we cannot simply apply them to our own situation, but they are nevertheless a powerful reminder that God is judge and that those who flout him will perish. Our problem in the comfortable West is that we do not often empathize with those who live in communities ravaged by war and violence.

Chapter 3 is plainly the pivot of the book of Lamentations. We are never again to reach a point as high as verses 21–39. While such a leap of faith is not to be made again (although see commentary on 5:19, 21, pp. 196–197), it colours the rest of the book. We cannot read chapters 4 and 5 as if they were simply a repetition of chapters 1 and 2.

Moreover, the chapter as a whole is probing theological depths with its calling on the name of the Lord and its echoes of the Psalter. God has punished, yet the poet refuses to let go of God. This man has travelled the journey himself, so he can speak for others. We have already noticed the blend of 'we' and 'I' language; it is personal but not private, and the poet longs not only for his own rescue but for that of the whole community. He wrestles with the situation to find what God, the God of his ancestors, is saying in these circumstances. Like Jacob (Genesis 32:26), he will not let God go until God blesses him.

REFLECTION

Experiences of darkness are not ends in themselves but opportunities to enter more deeply into a relationship with God.

TARNISHED GOLD

It is worth pausing to consider the place of chapters 4 and 5 within Lamentations. Chapter 3, as already noted, is the pivot of the whole book, and the subsequent chapters are more reflective and sombre. Chapter 4 is close to chapter 2 in both outline and events, but contains more analysis of what went wrong. The poet contrasts the former splendour of the city with its current pitiful situation.

Tarnished gold

'How the gold has lost its lustre, the fine gold become dull' (v. 1). Gold was, of course, the most precious metal in the ancient world, but there is more to it than that. Gold was a material extensively used in the building of Solomon's temple (see 1 Kings 6—8). In Paul's words about the temple of God (1 Corinthians 3:10–17), it becomes a symbol of what is lasting and durable in God's sight. The gold has proved to be dispensable in Solomon's temple, and is now cast aside. Without taking the analogy too far, the fact that it is still gold, though tarnished, could possibly suggest that there is still a future for the people.

Inhuman behaviour

From verse 3 onward, we have a grim picture of famine and of the terrible behaviour of the starving people. This culminates in verse 10: 'With their own hands compassionate women have cooked their own children'. Judgment is comprehensive in its devastating effects on the whole of life. The poet laments that the city's punishment is greater than that of Sodom (v. 6), which was destroyed quickly rather than suffering the lingering agony of Jerusalem.

Now and then

The contrast between the city as it is now and the glories of its past are described in vivid pictorial language. Verses 3 and 4 recall Isaiah's picture of pre-exilic Israel, which sees the city as an affront to the natural order (Isaiah 3). There the city was prosperous and luxurious; here it is a ruin. This shows that spiritual as well as physical decay is envisaged—a comprehensive breakdown of national life. Verses 7 and

8 use language about the human body in a way reminiscent of the Song of Songs, but with a very different purpose. There the writer celebrated the beauty and wonder of humanity—fallen indeed, but still in the image of God; here the appalling inhumanity is sketched.

All this is related to the concept of covenant, with the blessings that follow obedience and the curses that follow disobedience. The description here is close to what is said about covenant curses in Deuteronomy 28:15–68. Indeed, the eating of children is specifically mentioned there in verses 53–57. The author clearly sees what is happening as a result of the curses following upon disobedience to the covenant.

What we have in chapter 4 is thus a more theologically weighted reflection on the exile, yet it is far from abstract theology. The pain is too great and the experience too intense for that. The author is painting a word-picture of how judgment is experienced, drawing us into that grim world by poignant and memorable language. The commentary on the Song of Songs emphasizes that love makes us more truly human. Here violence, war and deprivation make us less so. There is much to be learned from reading these two books together and seeing the complementary emphases of their theology. What we have here in Lamentations is the ultimate result of human fallenness and rebellion.

PRAYER

Lord, give us courage and realism as we face the darkness of our own hearts and turn to you, who alone can forgive and heal.
Amen.

WHY DID IT HAPPEN?

Here, more fully than elsewhere, the author dwells on the reasons why the exile happened. In particular, behind all the secondary causes is the anger of the Lord (v. 11). This catastrophe is punishment for sin, portrayed as being consumed by fire. The other reasons are explored as evidence of the anger of God.

The apostasy of the religious leaders

Prophets and priests who ought to have led the people in holy living and good teaching have led them to their downfall. The phrase 'who shed within her the blood of the righteous' (v. 13) may simply mean that, by their false teaching and bad example, they led the people astray and thus contributed to their destruction, although it may suggest more active persecution. The same charge is made against Manasseh in 2 Kings 21:16 and against princes and officials in Ezekiel 22:6–27. Those who misled others are now said to 'grope through the streets like men who are blind', and have become polluted with blood (v. 14). Bad leadership is both a cause of faithless people and, by means of a vicious circle, the result of such a community. The nation, called to be holy, is now an outcast and leper among the nations (v. 15). The people have become like the scapegoats of Leviticus 16: wanderers and exiles. Once again, this is no random chain of events: 'The Lord himself has scattered them' (v. 16). The actions of the opposing nations are the actions of God himself. Priests and elders are now despised, and rightly so, in view of their own apostasy.

The ferocity of the enemy

Another factor in the disaster was the overwhelming nature of the opponent: the Babylonian army: 'Our pursuers were swifter than eagles in the sky' (v. 19). Wherever the people fled, there was no escape. This was true of inhabited places—'our streets' (v. 18)—but also of lonely and desolate country: 'they chased us over the mountains and lay in wait for us in the desert' (v. 19). The power of Nebuchadnezzar of Babylon is emphasized in verse 17: 'from our towers we watched for a nation that could not save us'. The 'nation' being referred to is almost certainly Egypt. Long past its greatest days, that country was unable to help them against the might of Babylon. Their hopelessness is underlined in verse 20, where the fate of Zedekiah, the last king of Judah, is described poetically: 'The Lord's anointed, our very life breath, was caught in their traps' (v. 20). The 'shadow' of the king is a metaphor for his protection, often used of God himself in the Old Testament (for example, Psalm 17:8). The apparent end of the Davidic dynasty spelt the end of their hopes as a nation.

A word of grace

The night is black, but a star is shining: 'O daughter of Zion, your punishment will end; he will not prolong your exile' (v. 22). The people of God will be restored. This is said in the context of an attack by the Babylonians on Israel's near neighbour, Edom. The prophecy of Obadiah (especially vv. 11 and 12) speaks of Edom's gloating over the destruction of Jerusalem. She will herself suffer the same fate, however, and her rejoicing will prove to be short-lived. The 'cup' is a metaphor of God's anger and will lead to drunkenness and exposure (v. 21).

Zion will be restored, however, and in verse 22 we have the first unambiguous note of hope in the book. Judgment was severe and deserved, but the repentance and confession that lie at the heart of Lamentations have helped to prepare the way for the possibility of a new dawn.

PRAYER

Lord, we ask for grace to face up to the darkness in our hearts, in our churches and in our communities. Give us hope for the future.
Amen.

'REMEMBER, O LORD'

The final poem is a powerful and eloquent one with echoes of such community laments as Psalms 44 and 74. It is a communal prayer, perhaps said at the site of the temple mound (see v. 18). The chapter divides naturally into two parts, of which the first (vv. 1–18) is our concern here. We have a final and deeply felt summary of the situation, with an appeal to the Lord in verse 1 which is echoed in the final section (5:22). The poet introduces a number of important themes as we near the end of the poem.

Appeal to God

'Remember, O Lord' (v. 1). The word 'remember' is a rich biblical one. This is not a prayer for God merely to recall something, as if he has forgotten; rather it is an appeal to him to act decisively. Two striking examples elsewhere in scripture are 'God remembered Noah' (Genesis 8:1) and 'God... remembered his covenant with Abraham, with Isaac and with Jacob' (Exodus 2:24). Both of these verses are introductions to decisive action and to a radical change of situation. Here in Lamentations, the situation is described as 'our disgrace', and this, combined with the use of 'Lord', the name of the covenant-keeping God, is a powerful call to reverse what has happened.

Loss of identity

'Our inheritance has been turned over to aliens' (v. 2). The word 'inheritance' is used in, for example, Deuteronomy 4:38 to mean the promised land, and this reminds us that the exile was seen as a reversal of the exodus. The promise of land goes back beyond the exodus and is part of God's covenant with Abraham. Here, as in so much of the book, the loss of identity and the sense of alienation are powerfully expressed.

Degeneration into chaos

These verses are masked by sober realism as the community sees the destruction of everything that ordinary life offered. Life is unbearable, as the comparison to widows and orphans shows (v. 3). The people have no control over basic resources (v. 4). The natural order is overturned, with slaves ruling (v. 8). There is oppression and cruelty, and even the dead are dishonoured. 'Princes have been hung up by their hands' (v. 12) probably refers to the desecration of corpses. The community has collapsed, and all rejoicing and gladness has gone. In the midst of this misery, verse 7 is important: 'Our fathers sinned and are no more, and we bear their punishment.' This is in keeping with the theology of Exodus 20:5 and contains the idea of community solidarity. It does not mean that the present generation is innocent, but that their sin is a culmination of centuries-old rebellion.

Destruction of Zion

Summing up and superseding even these horrors, however, is the fact that 'Mount Zion lies desolate' (v. 18). Zion was the very heart of Israel's life and worship. There, Solomon, at the height of both his power and spiritual maturity, had celebrated the completion of the temple (1 Kings 8) and Psalms such as 48 had extolled its beauty as the place where God dwelt and from which he shone. This beautiful place is now the haunt of jackals. Ironically, Isaiah (13:21) had prophesied such a fate for Babylon, which God was to judge.

The very fact that the community is at prayer is a sign of deep repentance. There is a recognition that the people's sin is an age-old problem and yet that they were also personally responsible. This is to lead to the concluding section, which is likewise marked by sober realism.

PRAYER

Lord, remember us in our sinfulness and bring us back to yourself.
Amen.

IN YOUR ANGER, REMEMBER MERCY

These final verses of the book strike two notes: one celebrates the eternity of God and the other emphasizes the need for repentance. Thus there are both certainties and questions, which are always part of the life of faith. What has happened cannot be solved by a few soundbites, and there are still many painful lessons to be learned. Memory, as we have seen, has been a powerful strain both in this chapter and throughout the book, and the recollection both of God's presence and the unfaithfulness of the people has been a major theme.

Conviction of the reign of God

Mount Zion may be desolate, but God's throne remains and his kingdom has not been overthrown. Verse 19 is a statement of faith that, like many parts of Lamentations, echoes the Psalter, such as Psalm 102:12: 'But you, O Lord, sit enthroned forever; your renown endures through all generations.' That Psalm continues with the assurance that the Lord will restore Zion. A group of Psalms such as 93, 96, 97 and 98 are often called 'enthronement' psalms, and celebrate Yahweh's kingship. That kingship is often seen against hostile powers, such as the raging waters (Psalm 93:3-4).

In the context of Lamentations, this is more than a simple repetition of one of the central affirmations of Israel's faith. It is a note of praise, and of confidence that the present crisis has left God's kingship untouched. Nothing that has happened has altered God's sovereignty in any way. This is faith trusting in the great realities of God's loving purposes when everything around seems to deny them.

Questions remain

Such strong faith is not incompatible with worries and questions about the community's own future. The opening 'remember' (5:1) is now underlined with a question about why God forgets and forsakes (v. 20). Of course, God has judged and rejected his people; that is what the exile is about. The question is whether this rejection is permanent.

Next comes yet another realization of the necessity of repentance:

'Restore us to yourself, O Lord, that we may return' (v. 21). This is a powerful reminder that repentance itself must be initiated by God and must result in a true turning to him by his people. The further phrase, 'renew our days as of old', is a plea for a return to the days of the nation's youth, when the Lord made a covenant with her.

The final verse leaves the outcome of the situation uncertain: '…unless you have utterly rejected us and are angry with us beyond measure'. This uncertainty is a reminder that we cannot take God for granted. The poet has to keep on living with such questions. He will not presume on God or imagine that repentance is a cheap and easy way out.

Lamentations is not an easy book to read and study, but it is part of scripture and has important lessons for us. As we come to the end of our study, two thoughts sum up the road we have travelled.

The first is that this book is an important testimony to the power of memory and its significance in preserving a tragic but influential period in the life of the Jewish people. The exile was a watershed in their history and, at the time, appeared to end that history. Lamentations is a continual reminder not to take God for granted and to make sure that such a time may not be repeated.

Second, Lamentations is a book about repentance. This is the key that unlocks the door of despair. The land is desolate and the temple has been destroyed; the covenant appears to be null and void. The solution is to seek God earnestly and, like Jacob in Genesis 32, not to let him go until he blesses.

PRAYER

Lord, you have given us the whole of scripture for our learning. We thank you for the book of Lamentations and ask that we might learn wisdom from its difficult lessons. Amen.

NOTES

NOTES

NOTES

NOTES

NOTES

NOTES

NOTES

NOTES

RUTH, ESTHER, ECCLESIASTES, SONG, LAMENTATIONS

THE PEOPLE'S BIBLE COMMENTARY

VOUCHER SCHEME

The People's Bible Commentary (PBC) provides a range of readable, accessible commentaries that will grow into a library covering the whole Bible.

To help you build your PBC library, we have a voucher scheme that works as follows: a voucher is printed on this page of each People's Bible Commentary volume (as above). These vouchers count towards free copies of other books in the series.

For every four purchases of PBC volumes you are entitled to a further volume FREE.

Please find the coupon for the PBC voucher scheme opposite.

All you need do:

- Cut out the vouchers from the PBCs you have purchased and attach them to the coupon.

- Complete your name and address details, and indicate your choice of free book from the list on page 208

- Take the coupon to your local Christian bookshop who will exchange it for your free PBC book; or send the coupon straight to BRF who will send you your free book direct. Please allow 28 days for delivery.

Please note that PBC volumes provided under the voucher scheme are subject to availability. If your first choice is not available, you may be sent your second choice of book.

THE PEOPLE'S
BIBLE COMMENTARY

VOUCHER SCHEME COUPON

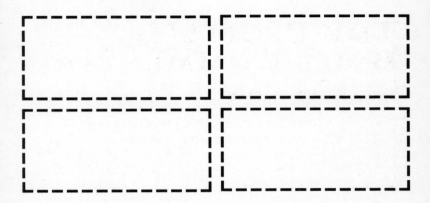

Customer and bookseller should both complete the form overleaf.

TO BE COMPLETED BY THE CUSTOMER

My choice of free PBC volume is:
(Please indicate a first and second choice;
all volumes are supplied subject to
availability.)

☐ Leviticus and Numbers
☐ Joshua and Judges
☐ 1 & 2 Samuel
☐ 1 & 2 Kings
☐ Chronicles to Nehemiah
☐ Job
☐ Psalms 1—72
☐ Psalms 73—150
☐ Proverbs
☐ Jeremiah
☐ Ezekiel
☐ Hosea to Micah
☐ Nahum to Malachi
☐ Matthew
☐ Mark
☐ Luke
☐ John
☐ Romans
☐ 1 Corinthians
☐ 2 Corinthians
☐ Galatians and Thessalonians
☐ Ephesians to Colossians
   and Philemon
☐ Timothy, Titus and Hebrews
☐ James to Jude

Name: . . . .
Address: . . . .
. . . .
Postcode: . . . .

TO BE COMPLETED BY THE BOOKSELLER

(Please complete the following.
Coupons redeemed will be credited to
your account for the value of the
book(s) supplied as indicated above.
Please note that only coupons correctly
completed with original vouchers will
be accepted for credit.)

Name: . . . .
Address: . . . .
. . . .
Postcode: . . . .
Account Number: . . . .

Completed coupons should be
sent to: BRF, PBC Voucher
Scheme, First Floor, Elsfield Hall,
15–17 Elsfield Way, Oxford
OX2 8FG.

Tel 01865 319700; Fax 01865
319701; e-mail enquiries@brf.org.uk
Registered Charity No. 233280

**THIS OFFER IS AVAILABLE IN THE UK
ONLY**
**PLEASE NOTE: ALL VOUCHERS ATTACHED
TO THE COUPON MUST BE ORIGINAL
COPIES.**